W9-COO-370

THE
CAREER
DOCTOR

Preventing, Diagnosing, and Curing
Fifty Ailments that Can Threaten Your Career

Neil M. Yeager, EdD

Illustrations by David Gordon

JOHN WILEY & SONS, INC.
New York • Chichester • Brisbane • Toronto • Singapore

In recognition of the importance of preserving what has been written, it is a policy of John Wiley & Sons, Inc. to have books of enduring value published in the United States printed on acid-free paper, and we exert our best efforts to that end.

Copyright © 1991 by Neil M. Yeager, EdD

Published by John Wiley & Sons, Inc.

All rights reserved.

Reproduction or translation of any part of this work beyond that permitted by Section 107 or 106 of the 1976 United States Copyright Act without the permission of the copyright owner is unlawful. Requests for permission or further information should be addressed to the Permission Department, John Wiley & Sons, Inc.

Library of Congress Cataloging-in-Publication Data

Yeager, Neil M.
    The career doctor : preventing, diagnosing, and curing fifty ailments that can threaten your career / Neil Yeager.
        p.   cm.
    Includes index.
    ISBN 0-471-54497-3. — ISBN 0-471-54496-5 (pbk.)
    1. Vocational guidance.   2. Career development.   I. Title.
HF5381.Y424   1991
650.1—dc20
                                                                    91-3497

Printed in the United States of America

10 9 8 7 6 5 4 3 2 1

ACKNOWLEDGMENTS

I wish to thank my wife, Cletha, for helping me develop the concept for this book and for keeping me balanced throughout this project. I'd like to thank Miriam Williford for her unwavering support of my writing. Much thanks to Judy Wardlaw for her editorial assistance and good ideas. My thanks to my editor, Steve Ross, for his confidence in and commitment to this project, to my illustrator, David Gordon, for his talented drawing, and to my agent, Elizabeth Knappman, for doing what she does so well.

PREFACE

For the past ten years I've spent a good deal of time in my work helping people prevent career problems before they occur, overcome mistakes when they've made them, and heal the wounds and ease the pain associated with career distress. Most important I've tried to help people thrive at work by helping them create the careers that they want.

The more time I spend in this business, the more aware I am of the complexity of managing that part of our lives that we call work. That's why I decided to write *The Career Doctor*. Many years ago I read a report suggesting that 80 percent of the population enjoys 20 percent of their work time. This means that four out of five people spend four out of five days a week doing things that they don't enjoy. By way of contrast, 20 percent of the population enjoys their work 80 percent of the time. In other words, the fortunate few spend four out of five days a week enjoying their work.

The moment I read that I decided my work in career management would focus on helping that 80 percent who are dissatisfied 80 percent of the time become part of the 20 percent who are *satisfied* 80 percent of the time. That is a tall order. What I have found over the years is that people can create work situations that provide them with what they want and need, but that career success and satisfaction do not come easily. Those who achieve the kind of success I'm talking about do so out of a relentless pursuit of those things that really matter to them. They don't find the best jobs—they create them. They don't react to problems—they anticipate and attack them. They don't accept failures—they learn from and make the most of them. They don't sit around waiting for things to get better—they seize the moment, create opportunities for themselves, and defy the odds against them.

It's exciting, challenging, and rewarding when you see someone move from a work life that is full of dissatisfaction, despair, and frustration to one that is full of excitement, enthusiasm, and optimism. In *The Career Doctor* I've tried to provide some strategies for prevention of career problems, some remedies, some prescriptions, and perhaps some antidotes. I've tried to emphasize the importance of creating and maintaining balance, as well as the importance of paying constant attention to and measuring your own levels and definitions of success. I hope that you resist the malaise of career despair that afflicts so many people and that instead you choose career wellness—and I hope that I help you get there.

Neil Yeager
Amherst, Massachusetts

CONTENTS

Introduction

The Career Doctor is the answer to your career problems—and your guide to career wellness. Whether your problem is psychological, strategic, or related to changes in your organization or the politics of career management, *The Career Doctor* can help you handle it. This book will help you identify problems, analyze them, figure out what went wrong, and come up with solutions that work.

Most successful people are pretty good at handling the basics of career management. What gets them into trouble is something unforeseen and unpredictable that throws their career off track. It might be a change in a key work relationship—or a change in their relationship to their work. It might involve the wrong approach to handling a tricky situation, or a change in the external environment over which they have no control. Perhaps they come face to face with a moral or ethical dilemma that they've never encountered before, or they realize in retrospect that they've made a poor decision or used bad judgment. It might simply be that their attitude toward their work has changed.

Whatever the problem, the key to career wellness is to recognize problems early, tackle them immediately, and eliminate them completely. By reading *The Career Doctor* you will become an expert at diagnosing, handling, and resolving any potential threats to your career. You will become skilled at anticipating, evaluating, and controlling changes so that they don't control you. Your career is a vital part of your life; it makes sense to take care of it.

THE DOCTOR-PATIENT RELATIONSHIP: WHY PLAY DOCTOR?

Managing the health of your career is a lot like managing your body. You need to take care of every aspect of it. You need to nurture it to avoid problems, and you need to pay attention to problems when they emerge. The longer you wait to respond to warning signals, the more complex the problems become. As you enter into the doctor-patient relationship with me, I urge you to take an active role in the management of your own situation. The best way for us to work together is as partners. You know yourself and your own situation best; I have information and insights to offer that can help you make informed decisions.

As we look at the many areas that require your attention, we'll focus on those kinds of problems that are most common and likely to be encountered by the largest number of people. Occasionally we'll look at unusual problems as well—things that happen less frequently but can be so devastating that they're worth our attention.

Ideally our relationship will be a preventative one—reading this book will help you avoid some of the common maladies that afflict many careers. When prevention fails, I hope to offer ways to rectify problems so that you and your career emerge intact. In that sense this book serves as both a primer for managing career complexity and a reference guide for overcoming threats to your surviving and thriving in what can often be a hostile environment.

THE PICTURE OF HEALTH: ACHIEVING CAREER WELLNESS

Just as each part of your body is affected by distress in another part, every aspect of your career is vulnerable when one aspect is in jeopardy. Although we will pursue each of the key risk areas in depth, it is important to remember that none of these situations exists in isolation. Just as your back will begin to ache shortly after you've sprained your ankle, your job performance—and your career potential—will be affected by organizational changes. Similarly, your ability to handle the politics of career management will have an impact on your career strategy and your sense of competence related to your career management.

Your career wellness depends on the careful management of a range of interconnected parts, just as your body's wellness relies on the smooth functioning of interdependent systems.

Just as a child is unaware that all these systems working in unison are what make a person tick, many people are under the mistaken assumption that their job is all there is to their career. In fact, the healthy career, like the life-sustaining body, requires careful attention to a variety of interrelated areas: psychological issues, strategic issues, organizational changes, political tactics, and job performance problems. Each of these areas presents potential threats to your career wellness and will be examined carefully in your visit with the career doctor.

Here's to a healthy career!

ONE

Psychological Threats to Career Success

Of all the potential obstacles to achieving success, none is more debilitating than the psychological ones—those conditions or states of mind that prevent the talented professional from getting the results he or she wants. Without a personal "psychology of success" in place, your career is vulnerable to many conditions that can sap your energy, impair your performance, and limit your potential. You need to develop strategies for preventing psychological threats from attacking your psyche and learn to combat them effectively when they hit. Being prepared to handle such things as lack of confidence, diminished interest, unreasonable expectations, and dashed hopes will make an enormous difference in maintaining and sustaining a healthy career psyche.

THE PICTURE OF HEALTH: PSYCHOLOGICAL CAREER WELLNESS

When you meet someone who has achieved psychological career wellness, you know it immediately. This person falls into that small group of people who enjoy 80 percent of what they do (no job is perfect). To the psychologically healthy professional, work is pleasurable, exciting, challenging, and fulfilling. One of the most striking things about these people is the tremendous amount of energy they have for their work— and the tremendous amount of energy they have after work. People with a healthy psychological base to their careers enter into psychological contracts with employers, a contract that says, "We are here for our mutual benefit. I will perform a service for you as long as it continues to be advantageous for both myself and the organization. Once the relationship ceases to be beneficial for either of us, we agree to terminate the relationship." Although this sort of psychological contract can never be written, this sensibility permits the career psyche to thrive and excel regardless of the demands placed on the individual or the organization. The nature of this contract can get confusing because it has become increasingly acceptable to be disloyal to one's organization. Instability caused by mergers, buyouts, and reorganizations has taught us that blind loyalty to an organization is foolish, given the organization's inability to return that loyalty. However, some people—particularly those prone to disloyalty—take this argument to mean that no level of commitment is necessary in this dog-eat-dog world. Those people are making a tragic mistake with profound career implications.

Although blind loyalty can get you in trouble, a lack of commitment to your organization can leave your career without a base. Your career wellness is linked to your ability to create and maintain a psychologically healthy perspective on your work, one that is based on reality. This perspective exists to the extent to which you feel the work you do is an appropriate match for your skills, interests, and goals, and to the extent that these things are consistent with the needs of the organization. Feeling appropriately challenged is also important, because without potential for growth there is no motivation to perform, and without that motivation there is no performance—or at best poor performance—and little or no satisfaction. And for the healthy career, satisfaction is the bottom line.

RECOGNIZING PSYCHOLOGICAL THREATS

If you pay attention to the right signals, your mind will let you know when a psychological threat is emerging. Feelings of doubt, insecurity, frustration, or fear are all signs that your psychological well-being is facing a challenge. The way you describe your work to others can clue you in to impending problems. Feeling a need to complain a lot is a strong warning, as is the desire to avoid work. Your body is a good messenger of disintegrating conditions. Unexplainable aches and pains can be a signal that your body is taking the brunt of your career dissatisfaction.

Dreams

One of the more interesting ways your mind can alert you to a psychological threat is through your dreams. Many of my career change clients report having vivid dreams about their struggles. One of my favorites comes from a man who for the past ten years ran a carpentry and home-building business. Prior to that he was a physics teacher. His dream took place the night after the first session of an eight-week career renewal workshop series. In this dream he found himself working in an old dusty carpentry shop. He was working on some sort of contraption that contained the substance mercury. He was handling the blob of mercury when it fell on the floor. Suddenly I appeared in the corner of the room with a hockey stick in my hands. He asked if I could help him get the mercury back onto the table. I said yes, came over, and very angrily swung the hockey stick at the mercury, smashing it into millions of tiny beads and dispersing it into the thousands of sawdust-filled crevices throughout the shop. In the dream he looked at me and shouted, "Why did you do that? Now I'll never get it back together!"

The dream told him that he was indeed ready for a change, was worried about the magnitude of his dilemma, and was concerned that I might not be able to help him "get it back together." As a result, we were able to address his fear, talk about his broad range of seemingly unrelated skills, and build a foundation for working together. Most important, we were able to establish that I could help him look at the many options before him, but that he would be the one to put his skills together in a new way.

Although dreams can be interpreted any number of ways, what's important is not necessarily the meaning of the dream but its function as a warning sign that something is wrong and requires your attention. Paying attention to all the subtle and not-so-subtle ways your body and mind tell you that something is wrong can help you tackle psychological threats to your career success when they're at their least damaging—that is, as soon as they begin to develop. The longer you wait, the more complicated and more difficult they are apt to become.

MIDLIFE CRISIS, BURNOUT, AND WORKAHOLISM: THREE MISDIAGNOSED AILMENTS

In popular culture there is a tendency to search for simple ways to understand complex situations. The popularity of TV talk shows, magazines, and newspapers that condense complex issues into half-hour bites and six-inch blurbs reflects this desire to simplify multifaceted problems. The same is true in the world of work when dealing with career problems. Terms like midlife crisis, burnout, and workaholism are embraced to describe phenomena that are difficult to understand. The problem with this approach is that the simple labels end up blurring the problems instead of crystalizing them.

Midlife Crisis

The term "midlife crisis" has become a convenient phrase for encompassing a broad range of phenomena. Middle-aged men who decide to leave their wives use it as their excuse. Women faced with the "empty nest" phenomenon clutch at it to explain their feelings of loss. People overwhelmed with the relentlessness of their work find midlife crisis a convenient way to describe their discontent. The problem I have with the term is that it blurs one's perspective by bundling a very messy set of circumstances into a neat little package. Volumes of psychological research tell us that human beings periodically experience crisis in their lives. The experience is normal, natural, and to some extent predictable. What is not so clear is how to predict when various crises are going to hit. Here is where I differ with the midlife crisis experts who suggest that we all go through similar stages at similar points in our lives. A 60-year-old woman who debates whether she wants to go to law school, a 30-year-old physician who feels he's gotten all he can out of a medical career, a 65-year-old retired professor who starts his own consulting company—all defy the norms of the midlife crisis, life-stage theorists. The concepts of midlife crisis and predictable life stages fit a static, homogeneous culture—not anything like the one we live in. Life-style patterns today are such that you find people of all ages going through all of life's stages at different points in their lives. Finding a clear-cut definition of the midlife crisis experience is like trying to find a relevant present-day definition of the typical American family. There just isn't one.

Although the term "midlife crisis" may be an oversimplification of a complex set of circumstances—and in fact has been challenged by some researchers as being a questionable phenomenon—it is broadly accepted that many people go through developmental stages that signal shifts in values. Social service workers who want to make more money, corporate fast trackers who want less pressure and more control, and working parents who want to spend more time with their growing children are all examples of developmental shifts that get grouped under the moniker "midlife crisis." What's important here is not finding a label to make you feel more comfortable with your shift in values but finding the means to diagnose what has changed so that you can focus your attention on an effective response to the value shift. So should you find yourself wondering, as many people do, if you are on the brink of this seemingly widespread phenomenon, ask yourself what's going on beneath the surface of your discontent and you'll be much better off than than you will be wallowing in the comfort of your midlife crisis.

Burnout

Like "midlife crisis," the term "burnout" serves as a convenient umbrella for a variety of conditions, in this case most often emotional states. People who experience burnout tend to be suffering from extreme emotional fatigue and may be overcome with anger, frustration, sadness, helplessness, or a range of other feelings. The problem with using the term as a diagnostic device is that all it does is tell you the result of the problem, not its source. As the word implies, the result is a state of inaction or deadness in response to one's work. This does little to help you get past the problem. Rather than finding solace in the fact that you are burned out and are therefore justified in being unproductive, you need to focus instead on the emotions at the heart of the condition and zero in on its causes. Figuring out how you feel in the state of burnout and what the cause of those feelings is—information overload, interpersonal stress, unrealistic expectations, or some other source—will bring you much closer to being reignited than will simply focusing on being burned out.

Workaholism

The biggest problem with this term is its mixed message. When asked in an interview what their weaknesses are, many seemingly clever candidates respond, "I'm a workaholic." This response reflects the fact that the term, intended to indicate a negative addiction to work similar to alcoholism, is confused with an image that reflects being a committed, hard worker. People who use the term "workaholic" to describe themselves in a self-promoting way are confusing the ambitious, dedicated worker with the true workaholic, whose relentless pusuit of success leads to a life fraught with anxiety. The person who spends unreasonably long hours meeting unreasonable employer expectations may seem to be successful because of the external rewards they receive from those leading the way, but most recovered workaholics will tell you the crash is inevitable. When work becomes an addiction, the worker becomes dependent on the job. This dependency can take on many forms. Like other addictions, overdependence on work—and the striving toward success—leave a person feeling overly reliant on and victimized by the role they play in the world of work. With addiction comes an inability to make decisions, to see things clearly, and to be the master of one's own fate.

The term "workaholism" in its intended meaning can be helpful to describe a segment of the population that has actually developed an addictive relationship to work. If you truly believe you suffer from an unhealthy obsession with your work, you should seek professional help from someone who specializes in work-related disorders. The rest of us would do best to stay away from the term; like "midlife crisis" and "burnout," it only clouds the issue.

The point of all this is that, when faced with discontent, we often seek ways to categorize our dissatisfaction so that it feels less mysterious and less threatening. This only takes us further away from any real progress. In the rest of this chapter, I will confront some frequently encountered psychological threats to your career in what I hope is a more direct way than some of these diversionary tactics. I hope you choose this direct route with me as I believe deeply that it will bring you closer to the psychological health everyone needs to function optimally in a career.

LACK OF INTEREST

Symptoms

Boredom is the most telling symptom of this problem. Lack of interest in colleagues, projects, and the overall good of the organization can also signal that your career needs some attention. Feeling that the only things that matter to you are things outside the workplace is also a sign that your career needs some adjustment.

Diagnosis

The extent of the problem here depends on the scope of the disinterest. While no one can sustain a high level of enthusiasm all the time, a general sense of excitement, involvement, and investment in one's work is necessary for the healthy career.

The root of this lack of interest is often a value shift. A value shift occurs when people find themselves no longer caring about something that once held great importance for them. Value shifts are common occurrences in most people's lives. As mentioned earlier, they often get labeled as part of a "midlife crisis." Changes in a person's attitude about the importance of money, achievement, and recognition often reflect significant shifts in values.

Prognosis

While many people have developed coping skills for handling stress at work, many get thrown by the stress that accompanies indifference or lack of interest. If the indifference is the result of having to endure a negative situation for too long, then what's needed is a break from routine. There's a good chance that a vacation, a temporary reassignment, or even just a few days off may be enough to get you back in gear. If the indifference is the result of a value shift, chances are the remedy will take much longer, be more dramatic, and require a lot more energy.

Prescription

Whether a lack of interest in your work is a sign of radical change in your beliefs, or merely your need for a change in scenery is the first question to grapple with here. If it's the latter, what's required is a simple diversion—to allow you to return to work renewed. If it's the former, what's required is much more formidable and much more challenging.

Once you're clear about the root of the indifference, you can begin to combat it. One way to clarify the problem is to pay attention to the intensity of the discontent. The mild forms have a simple solution. Take a break. Whether it's long or short, away from the workplace or just down the hall depends on the parameters of the situation and the options available.

The important thing is to make yourself take the break and get some relief.

The indifference that accompanies the more severe forms of this condition requires much more complicated action. My first prescription for conquering your lack of interest is to be careful that you don't seek solace in that vague condition we call "midlife crisis." It may comfort you, but it won't help you very much.

What you need to do is search for the value shift that is causing your indifference. Some classic shifts include middle-aged men who wake up to the fact that they are strangers to their 16-year-old children, middle-aged women who find they are no longer interested in paying the price necessary to "have it all," devoted human service workers who are weary of living near the poverty level in order to help humanity, and corporate zealots who are tired of proclaiming that their company's product or service is superior to all others. These are just a few of the more common experiences that might trigger a loss of interest in one's work. They are profound changes in that once they are faced they present something of a Pandora's box. Going on becomes difficult because what has driven you in the past no longer holds its value.

The best thing you can do if your lack of interest is based on the kind of shift in priorities I've been talking about is to confront it head-on. Be honest about what needs to change. Don't tell yourself, "Maybe I'm just having my midlife crisis!" Accept that your life is in need of change and make the change no matter how painful. If you don't, you'll just be prolonging your misery. Remember, people don't get over a real crisis— they work through it.

LACK OF CONFIDENCE

Symptoms

This dilemma can present itself in a variety of ways. It can be an overall sense of doubt or can be related to a particular set of tasks or circumstances. Here we will be discussing it in its less severe, although potentially debilitating form; later in this chapter in "The Imposter Syndrome," we will discuss it in its broader form.

When we are looking at psychological threats to career wellness, it is helpful to think about a phenomenon called "self-talk," a term psychologists use to describe the messages people send to themselves about who they are and what they perceive. It is what you say when you're talking to yourself. In this context, we are talking about what you say to yourself that fosters a healthy or unhealthy career perspective.

Lack of confidence self-talk sounds something like this: "I can't do this job. I'll never finish on time. Can I really complete this project? I don't know what I'm doing," and so on. If you hear yourself saying these things to yourself you may be on a lack of confidence spiral downward.

Diagnosis

The first thing you need to do is figure out where the doubt is coming from. Is it a crisis of confidence or a crisis of competence? If it's really a question of confidence, then all you need is an attitude adjustment. The important thing is to figure out what's driving the doubt. Is it past experience, fear of the unknown, time pressure, the complexity of the task, or some other factor that's causing you the doubt? Figuring out the source of your lack of confidence will get you on to the road to recovery.

Prognosis

If your lack of confidence is based more on your feelings than on the reality of the situation, chances are good that a shift in perspective will help clear up the problem. If, however, the lack of confidence is tied to a real lack of ability to perform the task, your surviving the situation and avoiding a downward spiral will depend upon your ability to make tangible changes that result in a change of attitude.

Prescription

The first thing you need to do is determine whether you have a rational reason to doubt your ability to perform the task. The best way to do this is to do a quick history check. Is there anything in your background that suggests you can complete the task? Finding such evidence and thinking about it—or better yet writing or talking to someone about it—can diminish your lack of confidence. Pinpointing what in particular scares you about your ability to complete a task can also help. Once you've pinpointed the problem, the best thing to do is to take some action. If lack of information or knowledge is the problem, negotiate a way to get the data you need. If a time crunch is the problem, negotiate a change in timeline or a reduction of other duties to create more time for this project. If the task is too complex, ask for help. Each of these alternatives is better than moving forward with a lack of confidence, and any employer worth working for will prefer these alternatives to not getting the job done.

Lack of confidence often impairs one's judgment. Those who doubt their own competence develop an inability to ask for what they need, even when what they need is perfectly reasonable. An extended deadline, support staff, or access to information can make the difference between feeling overwhelmed by a goal or in control of reaching that goal.

One strategy for conquering lack of confidence is the Action Rule: When experiencing a lack of confidence, take action—any action—to increase your confidence. Here's a simple example. I once worked with a woman whose lack of confidence in her ability to get a job was so strong that she had stopped applying for any. Whenever a job prospect emerged, she would come up with a variety of reasons for why she wouldn't get it. After several attempts to break her of the negative self-talk she had patterned for herself, I gave up trying. Then I remembered the Action Rule. In our next session I told the woman that I wanted to stop *talking* about applying for jobs; instead, I wanted to spend our time together *applying* for jobs. Prior to our meeting I had gotten a listing of job openings that I thought she might qualify for and had them with me. When I showed them to her, she began her usual litany of why she would not get any of them. I interrupted her and restated my desire to spend our time applying for jobs instead of talking about why she was not applying for them. She still resisted, but I was insistent. I sat down at the typewriter and started writing a letter of application for her. Eventually she reluctantly joined in to compose the letter. When we were done, I stamped and addressed the envelope and handed it to her. We then walked down the street to the mailbox and I watched her hesitantly place the envelope in the box.

The walk back to my office astounded me. The woman began talking about how good it felt to finally get unstuck. She started talking about how great it would be if she got that job. By the time we got back to my office, she was asking to see the list I had. She spent the rest of the day typing letters and walking down to the mailbox each time a letter was finished for what now had become a symbolic journey. By the end of the month, her confidence was up, she had had several interviews, and she was considering several offers.

What happened for this woman was a simple phenomenon. The act of placing that first letter of application in the mailbox injected a ray of hope where there had been none. By simply applying the Action Rule, we were able to turn a hopeless situation into one with enough hope to get her back on track.

While the simple remedies outlined in this story may leave you doubtful about the power of the Action Rule, I assure you it works. Over the past ten years I have seen it work for countless participants in my Career Renewal workshops. Many participants come in for an initial consultation. They often leave the session signing up for the program. When they come in, they are distraught and confused. After signing up, they immediately change their demeanor and appear dramatically more optimistic. I'm convinced that what changes their mood is the fact that they have signed up to take action. Even though they are no better off than they were when they walked in, the act of signing up for what they hope is the first step to a more satisfying career turns them around.

SETTING YOUR SIGHTS TOO HIGH

Symptoms

Picture this: You've been reasonably successful in your career, yet you regularly get an image in your mind that you're running alongside a train and just can't seem to get on board. You may be the victim of this next malady. There's nothing wrong with having ambitious goals, but if you find that your reach consistently falls short of your goal, you may find yourself demoralized, dissatisfied, and demotivated.

Diagnosis

The first thing you need to look at is whether you have unreasonable expectations for your own performance. We are constantly bombarded with images via television and in particular the movies that suggest that it's easy for anyone who wants to rise to the top of a profession (the old American Dream idea). Just as buying a house—once thought of as the sign of success— has eluded the grasp of an increasing number of middle-class families, access to the top jobs in many companies has disappeared as the ranks of middle managers gets more crowded and the number of vice presidencies shrinks. What this means for many is that there needs to be a redefinition of success—one based in reality and not in pie-in-the-sky pre-programmed Hollywood terms.

Prognosis

It's important to test our perceptions against reality. People who tend to have the most trouble with this problem are the romantics—those of us who prefer to resist the harsher realities and embrace the Hollywood image. For the hopeless romantic, setting one's sights too high may very well be a lifetime occupation. People who can escape the temptation of self-delusion will have a much easier time facing the fact that enormous success comes only to those who work hard relentlessly, learn from their mistakes, and experience an unusual amount of luck. The rest of us can expect a moderate amount of success for our efforts, given the ever-changing environment and the intense competition in just about every field. There is nothing pessimistic about this view, although the romantic will undoubtedly think so. It is a view grounded in reality. It does not preclude exceeding our goals; it merely points us toward setting and achieving realistic ones. If our results exceed our goals, all the better.

I know about this personally. When I set out to write my first book, I intended to write a best-seller, so much so that I became paralyzed by the task and the odds against my succeeding. When I modified my goals and set out to write good books that sold reasonably well, I became far more prolific. This book is my third in three years. My books have done well and have opened many doors of opportunity previously unavailable to me. Had I waited for all the rare factors to line up that are necessary for that one-in-a-million opportunity, I'd still be waiting—and unpublished.

Prescription

Create reasonable expectations for yourself. Aim high but be sure your goals are within your grasp. Stretch yourself to go beyond current levels of performance, and do some reality testing periodically to make sure that what you're trying to attain is attainable. Most important, take the time to enjoy and appreciate your successes before you look around the corner for the next challenge.

RESTING ON YOUR LAURELS

Symptoms

Just when you get yourself to the point where you think things are going well in your career, the rug gets pulled out from under you. Suddenly you find that all your past successes are deemed irrelevant by those who count, and you're suddenly on shaky ground. Another symptom, and another twist on this phenomenon, involves a distinct feeling that you've outgrown your position, but things have gotten too comfortable for you to be motivated to move on.

Diagnosis

What you're experiencing is one of two phenomena that can be brought on by the dramatic acceleration of the rate of change in recent years. The first involves getting pushed out of a job because you haven't adapted quickly enough. If you look at any of the major gauges by which we measure the impact of time, you'll find that everything is moving much faster than ever before. Scientific changes, political changes, and technological changes happen in a fraction of the time they used to. Some say that what used to take five years now takes six months. What this means for your career is that any accomplishment, no matter how impressive, quickly gets buried in the time crunch; unless you continue to produce consistently, you run the danger of getting lost in the shuffle. The other phenomenon related to this problem is more of an internal problem, specifically, recognizing that your tendency to rely on your past success rather than pursue new challenges is a sign that you've outgrown your position and need to make a change.

Prognosis

This phenomenon can serve as a litmus test for whether you're in the right line of work. If, for example, your efforts to deliver on a given project leave you totally drained and exhausted, you could be in trouble. If you're banking on your extraordinary performance on one project to carry you on the job, you're headed for the outplacement office.

If, instead, you're merely making the mistake of being a little cocky by thinking your success gives you the right to take it easy for a while, chances are much better that you can overcome the problems brought on by resting on your laurels. This may not at first glance seem like too big a problem; however, there have been many casualties of this phenomenon. People make the mistake of thinking that they become inherently valued by their organization because of their proven potential to deliver results. What they don't realize is that in today's competitive environment what matters is not potential but ongoing results. In spite of all the attention being paid to the value of human resources and to recognizing people for their accomplishments, it is as true as it's ever been that the bottom line is still the bottom line.

Prescription

If the source of the problem is that you put your all into a project, did an incredible job on it, and consequently have little enthusiasm left for the product or service that you deliver, then resting on your laurels can be very dangerous. A lack of energy after the completion of a major project (precluding a reasonable breather) is a sign that you've used up your enthusiasm for that work and it's time to move on. The danger comes in thinking that your history of stellar performance will carry you for a while. Most likely it won't. If you've still got some investment in your work, you'll find that you can leave past successes behind and focus on creating new ones. If you're totally used up, you're better off getting out before your laurels shrivel and die, leaving you with nothing to show for your efforts.

WHEN YOUR JOB BECOMES A PSYCHIC PRISON

Symptoms

Perhaps one of the most debilitating of the psychological threats to your success is this condition, the psychic equivalent of being in prison. Feeling trapped by your current job can be devastating to your career. This feeling of entrapment can take many forms and can be brought on by such disparate factors as the people you work for, the people you work with, the structure of the organization, the product or service the organization provides, or the norms by which the organization operates. Regardless of its source, experiencing your job as a psychic prison can have a devastating impact on your career.

Diagnosis

The most telling sign of psychic imprisonment is an inordinate amount of worry. When worry becomes the prime focus of your work, you lose whatever chance for satisfaction that your job had to offer. I've seen this take many forms: a woman whose organization was shrinking became obsessed with the need to protect everyone from the inevitable changes they would experience as the result of the organizational shift; a man who hated his work but took solace in the fact that the norms of the organization were such that no matter how poorly he performed he knew he would always have a job; a man who hadn't taken a vacation in three years because he had been convinced that the organization could not function without him.

What drove all of these people, and other victims of psychic imprisonment, is fear. Fear of change, fear of instability, and fear of lack of control were some of the ways these people became imprisoned. Psychic imprisonment at work is insidious. It can be so subtle you might not even realize your sense of confinement until you're no longer confined. However, there will be signs that, if heeded, can clue you in on the problem and help you release yourself from its clutches. Reacting with an inordinate amount of stress at the prospect of going to work is a strong signal. Feeling a sense of dread, helplessness, or powerlessness are all signs that it's time to address the problem head-on.

Prognosis

In a curious way, people experiencing psychic imprisonment sometimes find comfort in their confinement. The woman who fancied herself the savior of the people in her organization, the man who found solace in his company's lack of response to poor performance, and the man convinced he was indispensable even for a week, came to find some way to value their otherwise restricting organizational lives. These interpretations of conditions that lead to a sense of false security can be deadly if not confronted. While psychic imprisonment is escapable, it most often requires a radical move—either a change in your relationship to the organization or a total break from the organization. Anything less is unlikely to help and could lead to a prolonged sentence.

Prescription

The reason psychic imprisonment is such a difficult problem is that, unlike real imprisonment, it's hard to realize you're imprisoned until you get out. Like real imprisonment, the result of prolonged incarceration gives you a sense of identity that's hard to give up.

In a critically acclaimed television role, James Earl Jones provides a revealing performance that can help us understand psychic imprisonment. In "Gabriel's Fire," he portrays a former police officer who's been incarcerated for more than 20 years. Due to a fluke in the system—and an ambitious attorney—he is finally and suddenly informed of his release. Although he abhors his incarceration, he has come to accept it and panics at the thought of living in the outside world. Once out he offers a poignant picture of a man struggling to adjust to life beyond the confines of the institution that had become his only reality. Although it's a struggle, he eventually learns to appreciate his new-found freedom and give up the limiting patterns he had been forced to accept as part of prison life.

While in reality no job can truly parallel the horror of life in prison, the results of psychic imprisonment can be debilitating and damaging to your career. Just as the character in the story was able to shed the oppressive trappings of prison, however, so can the constrained professional break out of the limitations of psychic imprisonment. Still, the task is formidable.

Take, for example, the three people mentioned earlier. The woman trying to protect everyone from the painful effects of downsizing eventually realized she was trying to do the impossible and left the organization to find a job where her role was more manageable and less self-defeating. The man hanging on to the security of the no-fault company moved on to a more exciting job in an organization that was far less secure but far more challenging. The man who, at the urging of his company, came to believe he had become indispensable moved on only to see the organization survive. The woman reports feeling much less stuck, the security-conscious man much more challenged, and the indispensable man far less burdened. Each left a position that had become, by its very nature, a psychic prison. By leaving a situation that felt confining and limiting for different reasons, they learned that their work and their lives had become constrained by the parameters that the organization set—and that they had bought into.

Here is the key to escaping the psychic prison. The reason it is such a powerful dilemma is that it involves a conspiracy of sorts. An organization enters into an arrangement with a worker in which both parties buy into a certain set of beliefs. These beliefs force the worker into a particular role that requires certain responses. When the needs of the organization and the potential for the individual are well matched, there is harmony and no need for escape. When the needs of the organization create demands on the individual that are either destructive or debilitating, the bars of the psychic prison appear and—for the health of the individual—they must be dismantled.

THE COMPARISON TRAP

Symptoms

Constantly finding yourself dissatisfied with your progress is the key sign of the comparison trap. In a competitive culture such as ours, we are constantly being enticed to compare ourselves to others. While conventional wisdom tells us it is unwise to compare ourselves to others, we seem unable to resist it. We base the quality of our children's schools on the comparison of student achievement scores to those at other schools. We judge our quality of life by comparing the size and location of our homes to those of our peers. We judge our career success by the size of our salary compared to those of others in our age group.

To some extent, the drive to compare ourselves to others is natural and healthy. What better way is there to gauge our progress? The problem occurs when we become obsessed with the success of others to the point where we cannot appreciate our own or when we bow to the pressure to meet some arbitrary societal norm established to measure success. Popular magazines regularly publish average annual salaries of various occupational groups to measure ourselves against. I can remember when it was said that the successful professional should earn his or her age times a thousand dollars—then it changed to twice one's age times a thousand dollars. If the trend continues, none of us but the very rich will have reason to feel successful. While establishing goals and finding role models who embody our ideals can help to clarify our direction, putting too much stock in these targets can lead to perpetual frustration.

Diagnosis

The best way to diagnose whether you are prey to the comparison trap is to take a moment to consider how much time you spend thinking about the achievements of your peers and the emotional intensity that accompanies those thoughts. Using peer progress to gauge your own progress is not a problem. The problem emerges when you find yourself dwelling on other people's successes and focusing on their results instead of your own efforts. If you find that other people's success motivates you to do more of what *you* want to do, you're in no danger (in fact, your career is quite healthy). If other people's success demoralizes, frustrates, or otherwise incapacitates you, you could be a victim of the comparison trap.

Prognosis

All of us compare ourselves to others. Some say it's human nature and thus inevitable. What matters is how we respond when confronted with someone who in our opinion has surpassed us and attained something we want. Like the person wanting to lose weight looking to someone of their ideal weight to inspire them, choosing someone who's achieved what you want to emulate is healthy. If the person you choose to emulate causes you to get depressed about your own weight—or your own success—you need to catch yourself before your entrapment leads to your failure.

Prescription

The key to freeing yourself from the comparison trap is perspective. When you find yourself comparing yourself to others in a self-defeating way, shift your perspective. Comparison is a very deceptive process. Frequently, the person you're letting undo your sense of self-worth has hidden circumstances relating to their accomplishments that are key to their success.

Quite often, these invisible factors have influenced what they've achieved. For example, people who have large financial resources available to them often can achieve certain levels of success more easily than those who don't. Another catch is that oftentimes successful people expend a great deal of time, money, and energy getting what they want. While it may look easy to an unknowing eye, you might very well be unwilling to pay the price this person has paid for success. Therefore, it is irrational that someone else's favorable circumstances would be the factor that prevents you from appreciating your own accomplishments.

The prescription for avoiding the comparison trap is—like many things—simple but not easy. In this case it involves turning conventional wisdom on its ear. Conventional wisdom states that you should not wear blinders and that you should take in everything around you to use as grist for the mill. When it comes to the comparison trap, my advice is to put your blinders on and keep them there. Instead of comparing your every move to the progress others are making around you, keep your vision narrow. Look at the past, the present, and the future, but don't dwell on other people's fortunes. There will always be someone around who is richer, thinner, has won more awards, done more things, solved more problems, and gotten more promotions than you. Why drive yourself crazy wishing you could change places with somebody else? More often than not, you probably wouldn't want to.

The important thing is to focus on your *own* progress, your *own* success. Gauge what you're doing now on where you want to be and draw your strength and stamina for future success on your achievements of the past and present. As long as you can look back and say, "I've come a long way from where I've been," you need not worry about how others are doing. If you cannot feel good about what you've done, that's another problem—one to be looked at later. The important thing here is not to let your illusions about other people's apparent victories—in what most critics agree is an all-too-competitive culture—tarnish your self-image and leave you with an unwarranted lack of self-esteem.

THE IMPOSTER SYNDROME

Symptoms

The imposter syndrome has been widely researched. It concerns some people's tendency to experience an unwarranted view of themselves as fakes, phoneys, and charlatans. Victims of the imposter syndrome experience an inordinate amount of self-doubt and self-questioning. It can be triggered at any time but is particularly debilitating when it occurs at critical junctures in one's career management. In its milder form, it shows up in self-deprecating conversation, downplaying one's strengths and accomplishments, and generally negating one's competence. In its strongest form it can create a sort of psychological paralysis; the victim is unable to perceive or articulate a sense of personal value.

One of the more serious places I see the imposter syndrome emerging is with people who change careers. Because changing fields requires a certain amount of self-promotion, the process gets intensified if the tendency for the imposter syndrome is present.

Diagnosis

Like many conditions, the imposter syndrome can manifest itself in a range of intensities. In its mildest form the person sends messages about personal accomplishments that say, "Anyone could have done it," "It was nothing," and "I had a lot of help with it; I really couldn't have done it by myself."

While those messages can hurt your chances in an otherwise positive situation, they are not nearly as damaging as the more severe forms. In its most severe form, the imposter syndrome leaves its victim with a gnawing feeling of incompetence and a compelling need to broadcast it.

Prognosis

The key to conquering the imposter syndrome is to identify its source. The milder forms are often the result of a lack of confidence brought on by taking risks and exploring new alternatives. Given the proper support and perhaps some coaching on presentation, it can be overcome. The more serious forms of the imposter syndrome require more complex interventions and will depend on the sufferers' willingness and ability to delve deeper into their own psyches to get at the root of the problem.

Prescription

For the milder cases I prescribe a three-stage process: reflection, introspection, and projection.

The first step is reflection. Looking into your past can provide fuel for diminishing doubt and overcoming insecurity. For example, when I experienced doubts about my ability to write this book, one of the most helpful things I did was to browse through my previous two books. I'm proud of both of them, and both received good reviews. This quick review of past success gives me the confidence to continue with my current project.

The second step is introspection. Here is where you need some honest conversation with yourself about your motivations and aspirations. Are your goals on the path you've chosen ambitious yet realistic? If your choices target something that is attainable given your history, determination, and willingness to pursue the unknown, then you've made a good decision and need to keep moving forward with confidence in spite of your doubts.

The third step is projection. Here you should mentally conjure an image of the end result as you envision it should be accomplished. In my case I imagine this book complete, sitting proudly on the shelf with the other two (and more important, in your hands). This process of reflection, introspection, and projection should help you overcome any stalled progress that results from a minor case of the imposter syndrome.

As with any other condition, the more extreme cases require more demanding responses. Like the advice offered the workaholic earlier, the extreme form of the imposter syndrome may require in-depth treatment with a qualified professional. Someone who suffers from a serious case of the imposter syndrome most likely has a problem with self-esteem. For the seriously afflicted, this poor self-esteem most likely has its roots in childhood. While some people can independently overcome the negative childhood messages that contribute to low self-esteem, many find it helpful to work the issues through with a professional therapist. What's quite often required to overcome the imposter syndrome is a rewriting of childhood scripts. Some experts in the field take the script metaphor further, suggesting that some people with poor self-esteem have been programmed to think that way and have what they refer to as "tapes" playing repeatedly in their minds. These tapes continuously replay the doubt messages that fuel the imposter syndrome. While erasing these tapes and replacing them with positive, self-affirming messages is difficult, it *is* possible, and the results can be a dramatic alleviation and perhaps even eradication of the imposter syndrome.

"IF I HAD ONLY . . ."

Symptoms

This problem deals with the psychological impact of regret. While some regret is inevitable in any ambitious career, problems emerge when regret becomes an overriding influence. As the heading of this section implies, regret becomes a problem when someone starts repeatedly declaring, "If I had only . . ." in response to their lack of career progress.

Diagnosis

In diagnosing this problem, it becomes important to determine whether a sense of regret is warranted or merely a diversion from the real problem. For some, genuine regret presents an opportunity to learn from their mistakes. For others it is a distraction from the reality that they are involved in a negative career pattern and need to make some changes in their current and future actions. The tricky thing about the "if I had only . . ." tack is that it can become a convenient way to rationalize a series of poor decisions. While there is nothing to be gained from dwelling on past mistakes, blind pursuit of the wrong goals can be problematic. Constructive reflection on past behavior can be a useful exercise that leads to some regret but nevertheless encourages action. Persistent regret can lead to a sense of hopelessness and self-pity that will only enhance the likelihood of more of the same in the future.

Prognosis

Regret can serve a useful function in your psychological career health if you heed its call and learn from your mistakes; such insights can result in renewed perspective and increased determination for future success, making it unlikely for regret to resurface in the future. If you let regret get the upper hand, however, demoralization and despair are likely to result, leading to a further sense of failure.

Prescription

The next time you find yourself saying to yourself, "If I had only . . ." stop and examine the reaction this statement elicits in you. If your reaction is fear and discouragement, you're probably creating more problems for yourself than necessary. If your sense of regret causes inaction, the problem requires a psychological shift on your part. What's at stake here is more than your mood—it's your performance and consequently your success.

Let's look at a simple example of how regret can work against you in a job search. I spend a fair amount of time in my career consulting with people who came close to getting a position and then didn't get it. Many of these people demonstrate textbook "If I had only . . ." behavior. They convince themselves that they did something in the search process, usually in the interview, that prevented them from getting the job. The worst of them beat themselves up over the situation and create elaborate scenarios for why their response to a particular question put the nails in their coffin. They become so distraught over their theory as to why they didn't get the position that they become immobilized, and their subsequent interviews suffer.

I try to tell these clients that there's a good chance some other factor came into play, a factor over which they had no control—like another person's qualifications, connections, or experience. I suggest that the fact that they came close to getting the position is a sign that they're interviewing well and should continue to do so. Occasionally clients pursue follow-up interviews with near-miss jobs to find out why they didn't come out on top. They often find that the reason, as I suggested, had nothing to do with their interview performance. Sometimes they believe it, but those invested in the "if I had only . . ." theories never do. Those who *do* accept that they had no control over their fate are able to move on, leave their regrets behind them, and do well in subsequent interviews. Those who are invested in their regret wallow in it as other opportunities pass them by.

Another thing that happens is that people who are open to examining reality rather than clinging to misplaced regret find out that they are applying for the wrong positions or are missing key qualifications. In these cases abandoning regret in favor of finding ways to fill gaps in order to get what they want leads to increased satisfaction and the limiting of future regret.

Regret can be paralyzing in that it creates a sense of powerlessness, a feeling that if you had done things differently you would be better off. At its worst it becomes a form of self-destructiveness that leads to self-condemnation, based on your assumption that you used poor judgment. What's important to remember here is that any healthy career, by definition, involves some risk, and the presence of risk always involves the potential for regret at having made a poor decision. What strikes me most about people in the "if I had only . . ." mode is their sense of helplessness. While it is unlikely that any of us could go through life with absolutely no regrets, the important thing is to learn to use these regrets to create better conditions in our careers and our lives, and not as a means for self-hatred.

WHY YOU SHOULD HAVE A PERSONAL CODE OF ETHICS BEFORE YOU NEED ONE

Symptoms

The key to overcoming the "ethics problem" is prevention. With a solid personal code of ethics, you should have no problem handling ethical dilemmas as they emerge. Ethical decision-making is a psychological process; problems emerge when you're faced with an ethical dilemma and have no personal frame of reference on which to base a decision. The major sign that you lack a personal code of ethics is finding yourself not knowing what to do when faced with an ethical question.

Diagnosis

Ethical dilemmas often emerge without warning. They can be brought on by co-workers' actions, managerial initiative, organizational shifts in policy, or external forces. While there is no way to predict when an ethical problem will emerge, where it will come from, or what it will be, the magnitude of the problem for you will be determined by the extent to which you have established yourself as someone with unquestionable ethics.

Prognosis

The key to surviving ethical conflicts at work is psychological preparation—establishing within your mind and in the minds of those in your sphere of influence that you have a definite set of standards for your ethical behavior. The first step involves getting clear as to the limits and parameters of your personal ethics. The second step involves letting others know what those limits and parameters are. With a clear view of your own standards and a clear articulation of those standards to others, you should have no problems.

Prescription

Many types of ethical problems can emerge in the workplace. Your own behavior, the behavior of co-workers, the establishment and shifting of company policy, financial dealings, legal issues, and the handling of sensitive information are some of the key areas likely to create ethical challenges. It's a good idea to take each of these areas into account in formulating your personal code of ethics. What follows are some key considerations for you to think about when pondering the tricky yet critical ethics issue.

Sensitive Information   If you doubt that information can create ethics problems, consider the cases of insider trading in which traders used secret information to influence their profits and the profits of their clients. Availability of the right information to the wrong people at the wrong time can violate an ethical trust between those who have legitimate access to information and those who gave you that access. Sometimes that trust is violated inadvertently under the guise of confidentiality. The person who inappropriately shares information with someone not granted access to that information by formal channels is flirting with trouble.

A good rule of thumb is that when it comes to sensitive issues, there's no such thing as personal confidentiality. People who receive information they aren't supposed to have are too tempted to share it with someone else. If you want to stay clean in this area, you'll make it your personal business to keep private information private.

Legal Issues   It's amazing how often people equate ethics with legality. While in a just society one hopes that the law reflects the highest level of ethics, everyone knows that there are times when ethical issues challenge legal ones. Lawrence Kohlberg, a widely respected theorist on moral development, provides some good examples of ethical dilemmas that can challenge legal boundaries. In a classic diagnostic tool for assessing moral development, he tells of a poor man whose wife needs some lifesaving medication. The man has no money to pay for the medication and has unsuccessfully tried to get it by every legal means. In a desperate act to save his wife's life, he breaks into a pharmacy and steals the medication. The question Kohlberg poses is, "Did the man commit a morally justifiable act even though he broke the law?" According to Kohlberg's criteria he did, because at the highest levels of morality one values human life over the constraints placed on individual behavior by legal dicta.

While you may or may not agree with Kohlberg's premise, the point is that you cannot always rely on the law to guide your ethical decisions. There will undoubtedly be times when conflicting conditions will challenge your ethics. Having your personal boundaries clear in relation to the law will help you when you are confronted with this sort of problem.

Financial Dealings   As with legal issues, there are formal rules about dealing with money that provide general parameters. However, there may be times when you are tempted to violate the rules. As in the example of insider trading, at times the opportunity for financial gain may influence your better judgment. People get crazy when it comes to money. Conditions such as indebtedness, easy opportunity, and greed can cloud their judgment. Having a solid, unwavering set of standards for dealing with money will help you stay out of hot water and keep your ethics clean.

Company Policy When a company changes its policy in a way that has ethical ramifications, the level of internal conflict among employees can be profound. Imagine that your company suddenly informs you of its decision to develop a new product that yields toxic waste. You may or may not have concerns about this. However, if you are environmentally conscious, you may be faced with an ethical dilemma with results ranging from becoming an internal watchdog to leaving the company. While you cannot anticipate all potentially ethically challenging situations, you can establish some personal boundaries going in so that you're not totally unprepared when your company does something you have trouble living with.

Co-Worker Behavior Chances are good that if you work with other people, you will eventually run into a situation where you see someone else behaving in a way that challenges your personal code of ethics. While you want to be careful not to impose your standards on others, there are times when you may feel compelled to respond to behavior that is potentially dangerous. Incidents of drug or alcohol abuse can be particularly challenging, as can safety violations. Once again, you're better off establishing a personal policy prior to being faced with an incident than relying on your ability to make quick decisions under difficult conditions.

Personal Behavior This is probably the most manageable of ethics-related areas in that it's the only one over which you have total control. Setting clear standards for your own ethical behavior and keeping to those standards can serve as a base that can keep you out of trouble when other factors threaten your ethics.

ALL IN THE FAMILY: DYSFUNCTIONAL PATTERNS AND THEIR IMPACT ON YOUR CAREER

Symptoms

We bring our family patterns into the workplace. After observing many organizations struggle with interpersonal dynamics and talking with many people who have had irreconcilable differences in the workplace, I have found undeniably that people bring their behavioral patterns from home to work. Depending on your perspective—and your history—this notion could leave you indifferent, or it could leave you terrified. If you came from (or live in) a healthy, nurturing, supportive family where most of the interpersonal dynamics were (or are) rational, reasonable, and "normal," then the idea that family patterns get replicated in our organizations will not cause you concern. However, if you came from a dysfunctional family or are currently in one, you may find this thought alarming.

In reality, all of us need to be concerned. Whether or not you came from a healthy family or live in one now, odds are that some of the people in your organization did not or do not. If you don't understand family dynamics and the potential for manipulative, deceptive behavior, you could find yourself at a real disadvantage.

If you find yourself engaged in a relationship at work that puzzles you and are wondering why you can't clear things up, it may just be that you've stumbled into a situation where someone's family history or current family dynamics is getting in the way.

Diagnosis

There are times when all of us behave irrationally, when our emotions take over and supersede reason. This can be expected and is certainly no cause for alarm. What is cause for concern is when you get the distinct impression that someone you are dealing with on a regular basis is carrying more "emotional baggage" than the rest of us. By this I mean that you are faced with someone who seems to overreact to what appears to be nothing out of the ordinary. When there seems to be a pattern to their reactions—one that becomes increasingly predictable—there's a good chance you've run into someone whose family life or family history is influencing his or her behavior at work.

Diagnosis is tricky here because you have no way of really knowing what goes on in other people's families or whether they've had a history that was problematic. You certainly have no right to probe into that area just because someone works with you. What you can do is protect yourself from the consequences brought on by someone's playing out dysfunctional family patterns at your expense.

Prognosis

If you can recognize a dysfunctional pattern early, you can usually protect yourself from its detrimental effect. The key here is making sure you don't play armchair psychiatrist and try to straighten the person out. You have no business doing that, and chances are you lack the skill to do so effectively. What you have to remember here is that you can't save these people; you can only save yourself from their destructive impact. In the process you may help them get closer to getting whatever help they may need; however, you need to remember that your best tack is to protect yourself from becoming entangled in what can be a psychological minefield.

Prescription

Here's where a little knowledge can go a long way. Much has been written in recent years on two key concepts for recognizing and responding to unhealthy family behavior. First is understanding the nature of the dysfunctional family; closely tied to it is understanding the nature of codependence.

Consider the following profile acknowledged by most experts as characteristic of severely dysfunctional families: rigid rules and roles, family secrets, closed to outsiders, unclear personal boundaries with little personal privacy, a denial of conflict, resistance to change, and a lack of family unity, creating a sense of fragmentation. In contrast, consider the characteristics of a healthy family: flexible rules and roles, openness between members, respect for personal privacy and the nurturing of each person's sense of identity, openness to outsiders and to change, tolerance for and the resolution of conflict, and a sense of interconnectedness.

Although no family is entirely healthy—in fact each of us can probably find some aspects of the dysfunctional family present in our own—when several of these characteristics exist concurrently in a family over a long period of time, you have a truly dysfunctional family unit. If you find after reading this description that you identify with many of the characteristics in the dysfunctional family, you may want to shift your focus away from the problems brought on by co-workers' behavior and take an honest look at the impact of your family life on your own behavior. Although patterns can replicate themselves—dysfunctional families often spawn other dysfunctional families—there's no reason to assume you have a problem that needs changing. It's entirely possible that you could be living a psychologically healthy life even if your family background was problematic. If, however, the family you now live in fits the dysfunctional model, there's a good chance of your bringing some negative behavior into the workplace.

This brings us to the next key concept: what you can do to break patterns. Oftentimes a severely dysfunctional family has at least one member who has a serious personal problem. This problem could be alcoholism, drug addiction, a tendency toward violence, or some other major disorder. If you have one of these problems, you certainly need to take care of it before you can expect to see an improvement in your family life or your work life.

What many people don't realize, however, is that the other people in the family have a problem as well. The problem is often called "codependence." A codependent is a person who becomes indispensable to others by dysfunctionally supporting an active addict in his or her addiction. Many experts believe that codependents need to go through a process of recovery that is just as important to their mental health as treatment and recovery is to the addict. However, given the large number of people still suffering through active addiction in its various forms, it's safe to say that there are a lot of people walking around—perhaps working with you—who have not confronted their codependence. In fact, it's probably safe to say that many of these people are replicating their dysfunctional family behavior in the workplace.

A long time ago, while I was receiving some counselor training in family dynamics, I remember the professor saying that in family therapy the identified patient is often the healthiest person in the family. I remember being puzzled by the notion, but it makes a lot more sense now in light of what's been discovered about codependence. Many times people are entirely unaware of the impact of their own behavior on others—especially those people who don't suffer from the more visible problems like addiction. When dealing with someone who has developed a dysfunctional pattern like codependence, one needs to confront that person's behavior head-on. Like the codependent who protects the alcoholic or addict from being found out, it is easy in organizations to protect oneself and others from the dysfunctional behavior that gets played out everyday. Just as the codependent needs to stop protecting and confront the alcoholic in order to break the dysfunctional pattern, people faced with dysfunctional behavior need to confront it. This does not mean that you should accuse someone of having a dysfunctional family! That is totally inappropriate and will surely backfire on you. What it means is that if you study the nature of the dysfunctional family, you can learn to recognize unhealthy patterns of behavior and begin to confront those who are behaving inappropriately.

Considering what's been said about dysfunctional families, you might want to watch out for certain behaviors that could be warning signs and be prepared to respond. While dysfunctional patterns can get played out in an infinite number of ways, here are some guidelines for consideration:

1. When confronted with what seem to be rigid rules, challenge the rule maker into justifying the purpose of those rules.

2. When you find yourself being pressured to take on a particular role repeatedly, make efforts to deviate from that role when appropriate.

3. Avoid entering into agreements with others that require unnecessary secrets.

4. Encourage outside opinions whenever feasible.

5. Establish personal boundaries at work and insist that others respect them.

6. Address conflicts with others directly until they are resolved.

7. Encourage and support positive change in the organization.

8. Foster a sense of unity and togetherness between yourself and other members of your work unit.

While these recommendations are not intended as a formula for handling all situations, they will help you avoid playing into the destructive patterns of colleagues. Like the relationship between the addict and the codependent, you need to be careful not to feed into the dysfunctional behavior of those who bring that tendency into the workplace. The best thing you can do for someone who is repeating dysfunctional family patterns at work is to be intolerant of that behavior. Only then might the person seek the help they need to develop a more healthy work style—and only then can you get on with your work in a way that is healthy for you, your co-workers, and your organization.

TWO

Strategic Mistakes and How to Handle Them

Everyone makes mistakes. If you choose to have a dynamic career, as I hope you do, it is inevitable that you will make some errors in strategy. Whether your blunders occur in the job search, on the job, or in transition, the key to your survival is responding swiftly and appropriately. Whether your situation involves an error in judgment, a bad decision, or simply being in the wrong place at the wrong time, your ability to strategize carefully in order to undo a bad set of circumstances will make the difference between prolonged agony and rapid recovery.

THE PICTURE OF HEALTH: STRATEGIC WELLNESS

The strategically healthy career reflects a clear sense of direction along with a preparedness to handle unpredictable problems. Career strategy involves the development of solid skills for managing changes and the ability to respond quickly and appropriately when things go wrong. A person with a solid career strategy does not wait for things to go wrong before acting; prevention is the preferred approach. You experience strategic wellness when you sense that what you're doing for work is moving you in your desired career direction. At best, career problems are averted because of clear strategy. At worst, they are addressed quickly once they emerge and are alleviated in the simplest and most effective way.

Poor strategic wellness develops when problems are ignored, avoided, or minimized. A tendency to put personal career needs on the back burner in favor of responding to your organization's demands is a classic threat to strategic wellness. Abdicating responsibility for your own career through a misguided belief that the organization will take care of you is another, as is letting organizational threats to your success go unanswered.

The strategically well professional is in control, constantly acting to avoid problems, addressing them head-on when they emerge, and always keeping an eye on the ball.

THE INEVITABILITY OF STRATEGIC MISTAKES

If you're at all successful, no matter how careful you are, chances are that eventually someone will create a plan for you that you are not happy with. Success breeds expectations, and sometimes those expectations will create demands you don't want. Finding yourself accepting a promotion that derails your career plans is one example; staying too long in a position that you've outgrown because it's comfortable is another. Being able to recognize actions, both your own and those of others, that throw your career off track is the key to strategic success. Awakening to the fact that you've become too specialized or not specialized enough, realizing that you've taken a job you shouldn't have, or finding yourself in an organization whose growth plans don't include you, require actions that will influence your strategic health. Being able to anticipate and respond to such threats is the key to your strategic wellness.

WHEN YOUR NETWORKING IS NOT WORKING

Symptoms

One of the most powerful tools for your strategic wellness is the nurturing and maintaining of your professional network. The problem with networking is that it contains a hidden trap—it's a lot easier to do it poorly than to do it well. If you imagine yourself suddenly losing your job and can't think of at least ten people who could help you launch an effective search, your networking is not working as well as it should. While this lack of preparation can be a problem, it is not nearly as urgent a networking problem as actually finding yourself in need with no one out there willing to help. Like good friendships, good networks are hard to come by. The best time to develop them is when you don't need them. Feeling isolated, being disconnected from others, and lacking a sense of personal and professional community are all signs that you don't have an adequate network.

Diagnosis

The biggest problem for those without strong networks is that they don't understand the process of building and maintaining a network. A network is not something one comes by easily, yet many people, confronted with the pressures of the work world and in particular the career marketplace, think they can "get networked" quickly and effortlessly. For example, I recently had someone tell me that she doubted the potential of networking: "I tried networking last Monday and it didn't work." This woman obviously doesn't understand the complexity of effective networking.

There are two kinds of networking problems. The first is attitudinal—those who doubt the power and potential of effective networks. The second is behavioral—those who lack the skill to develop and maintain a network.

Prognosis

Effective networking patterns can easily be learned. The important thing is to realize which approaches work best for you. If you're committed to building and maintaining an effective network, you can learn how to do it well regardless of your personal style. Problems like shyness, discomfort, and awkwardness that can lead to stalled networking can be overcome. If you doubt the effectiveness of networking, the problem is more severe because it is unlikely that you will commit the time and energy required to build a network that works for you.

Prescription

Networking is a technology and like any powerful technology, it is complex. It requires careful strategy, implementation, and ongoing evaluation to remain effective. The most effective networks are multidimensional in that they take on lives of their own and contribute to your career in ways you are not even aware of. Like a web of interconnections, a dynamic network creates both intentional and unintentional links among a potentially infinite number of entities. It is not limited by geography, by your line of work, or by organization. A truly effective network grows constantly, reaping countless benefits for its initiator.

Delores from Dayton: A Case Study in Networking Delores was a museum curator in Dayton, Ohio. Her husband had just received word that he was being transferred to New England. Delores loved the arts and was concerned about her chances of getting the kind of job she wanted in a very competitive environment. Once she and her husband agreed to move, Delores knew she had better start exploring ways to uncover opportunities but didn't know where to start, as making contacts so far away would be difficult. The first thing she did was contact all the Midwestern groups that might be able to help.

Her first nibble came from the Midwest Museum Education Council, of which she was a member. One of the other members told her that a former member, a curator of an art musuem in Detroit, had just moved to western Massachusetts, Delores's target area, to take a position as museum director.

Delores contacted the man and he agreed to see her, although he mentioned that there were no openings at that time. They met and had a good conversation about the Midwest Museum Education Council, their mutual contacts back home, and the state of the arts in general. At the end of the conversation, he referred her to two additional people. The first person was the president of a local historical society, who was also a member of the board of the local museum. The second was the director of a local private school for the gifted, who it turned out was also on the board of the museum and the director of membership for the historical society. Based on the museum director's recommendation, both agreed to see Delores. Although the conversations went well, neither person had any current opportunities for Delores to pursue.

By this time Delores was quite busy talking to a variety of people, stemming from that one initial contact. However, she knew that the process was to some extent a numbers game and that she had better continue expanding her "net." She approached the arts placement director at a local college, who suggested she talk to some people at a Northeastern university because she had seen an ad for someone to manage an arts festival.

Based on this referral, Delores contacted the woman in charge of the arts festival at the university. The woman agreed to meet with her and review her resume. She was quite impressed but suggested that Delores in fact might be overqualified for the position. While they were meeting, the woman introduced Delores to the director of the Arts Extension Service, the organization sponsoring the festival. The director reviewed Delores's resume and agreed that she was overqualified. It was unfortunate, he said, that she had not appeared a week earlier. He had just completed sitting on a search committee for a coordinator of arts programs for the

Division of Continuing Education. The search had been unsuccessful in finding a suitable candidate and had been closed.

Before leaving his office, Delores chatted with the director about her search activities and discovered that he knew many of the people she had contacted. She learned, in fact, that he too was on the membership committee of the historical society.

Frustrated but not thoroughly discouraged, Delores went home to regroup. After meeting with her, the director of the Arts Extension Service spoke with his colleagues on the membership committee of Sturbridge Village Historical Society in Massachusetts, and they all agreed that Delores had a formidable background and would be a welcome addition to the local arts community. After talking with his friends, the extension director decided to pursue the possibility of reopening the search for an arts coordinator. He was successful and invited Delores to apply. She got the job and has since expanded it to include a variety of other responsibilities at the university. This spring she will be celebrating her ninth year in the position.

By the time Delores accepted the position, she had received two additional offers and was able to choose the job she wanted. After she got her job, she was able to help the college arts placement director who had helped her find herself a new job.

Delores personifies the opposite of the Monday morning networker I mentioned who expected instant results. She realized that the keys to effective net working are tenacity, persistence, and patience. She made her "net work" for her by following every possible lead, getting other people to work on her behalf, and treating everyone she met with the utmost respect.

A closer look at Delores's networking behavior can offer some solid guidelines for developing and maintaining an effective network.

- Start early, before your need for contacts is acute. The best time to develop your network is when you don't need it.
- Start with people you know. You never know the extent of other people's networks until you tap them. Don't get

caught in the "I don't have the right connections" trap. Chances are good that someone you know already knows someone you need to meet.

- Remember, it *is* a small world. Increased mobility and access to long-distance relationships through widespread communications technology have made the possibility of broad-based networks a reality.

- Pursue opportunities to talk with people for no other reason than to make them part of your network. Don't expect to get something concrete from everyone you talk with. If someone is willing to give you ten minutes, take it. You never know where it will lead.

- Look for common interests, contacts, and experiences with everyone you meet. Commonalities increase the likelihood of someone joining your network.

- Ask for referrals to other potential contacts every time you talk with someone.

- Don't rely on one stream of contacts. Expand your reach whenever possible.

- Let everyone you meet know who else you've been talking with. People are connected to each other in ways that you may not know. The time they spend talking to each other about you can be a real boon to your network.

- Never stop developing your network. It can lead to multiple opportunities that come from unknown contacts between those in your network for whom you are the link.

- Remember that effective network maintenance is a two-way street. Help others in your network get what they need as often as you can. Nothing solidifies networks more than the realization by those in your network that reciprocity is the result of their efforts.

If you find yourself resistant to the concept of networking, it could be an attitudinal problem. The two most common attitudinal blocks to building and maintaining an effective network are fear and cynicism. While following the networking guidelines can help you behave in a way that leads to stronger networks, if you don't really want to build a network, the problem is more severe. If you found yourself feeling overwhelmed by Delores's story, it may be that you are one of those people who finds the prospect of networking intimidating, and you may therefore find all sorts of reasons why it "isn't for you." If you find yourself turned off by the "it's not what you know but who you know" implications of networking, you're deluding yourself into thinking that your career will thrive on your merit alone and not on your connections. The only problem with this thinking is that you're competing with others who do use networks. You need to realize that if you want to compete on a level playing field, you need to develop a personal strategy for generating and using contacts.

There are many ways to overcome fear or shyness related to networking. One way is to start out by playing it safe. Think about people you know who would most likely respond favorably to your networking efforts. They might be relatives, close friends, or just people you find less threatening. Start building your network with these safe people, and pretty soon you'll find yourself venturing out toward more challenging relationships. In networking, success breeds confidence. The more successful you are in safe ventures, the bolder you will get and the richer your network will become. If you find the prospect of contacting someone really intimidating, start out with the least threatening type of communication, the written word. Write a letter to this person asking for ten minutes of time, explain why, and say when you will follow up with a phone call. This one-way communication allows you to say exactly what you want in the initial contact (which is often the most difficult), breaks the ice, and prepares the other person for the conversation. It also locks you into making the phone call because you said you would. Chances are if you get through to the person at all, you will find someone on the other end who's had a chance to think about the prospect of talking to you and has decided to do so. You can enter the conversation knowing the other person is willing to entertain the possibility of becoming part of your network. A word of warning: Don't say, as someone said to me recently, that he was calling because he wanted to "network me." I resented it and got off the phone as quickly as possible. Let people know why you have chosen them in particular and, if you can, why they might find talking to you interesting. Give them the possibility that they might have something to gain from the conversation—even if it's just a few minutes of good conversation—and chances are greater that you'll get the response you want.

If what's bothering you is that you don't like the idea of tapping your personal network for contacts or don't feel you have any worthwhile ones, here's an example of how you might start from scratch.

Joe Malone: From High School Teacher to Corporate Trainer
Joe Malone was a high school science teacher who, after 15 years, was tired of teaching science. He decided he wanted to become a corporate trainer but didn't know where to begin. He believed he didn't know anyone who could help him make the transition and felt uncomfortable pursuing possible contacts in his current circle of friends. Most of them were teachers, and his comments to them about leaving the field were met with disappointment bordering on hostility. Joe decided to start from scratch. He went to the library knowing nothing about corporate training. He asked the librarian if there were any journals on the subject. She found two, *Training Magazine* and *Training and Development Journal*.

He took them home, read them cover to cover, and found them very interesting. He got excited about breaking into the field and looked to find out who published them. When he discovered that *Training and Development Journal* was published by the American Society for Training and Development, he called the toll-free number listed in the magazine to find out if they ever held meetings. He found out that a national conference was coming up, and went, where he met some people from his city's chapter. They told him that the chapter held monthly meetings that featured dinner and a speaker.

Joe joined the chapter and started attending meetings. At these meetings he found himself surrounded by 50 to 60 people who held the kinds of jobs he was looking for. He learned from them what their priorities were, what their skills were, and what the work was like. Before long he started hearing about job openings and even got invited to apply for a few. By the time he found himself in job interviews, he had learned to "talk like a trainer and walk like a trainer." Most important he learned how to couch his skills in terms that would appeal to those in corporate training. He learned to call his curriculum development skills "program design skills," his administrative skills "managerial skills," and his teaching skills "platform skills." Most important, he learned to communicate to those doing the hiring that he had an appreciation for the bottom line—something his interviewers feared that teachers lacked.

Through the careful development of a new network—one started from scratch—Joe was able to establish a network of contacts quickly. It was one that led to a series of job offers that never would have come his way had he just done what most people do—answer ads in the newspaper.

STAYING TOO LONG IN A POSITION

Symptoms

There is an illusion in corporate America that longevity breeds security. While this may have been true in the "30-year gold watch" paternalistic organizations of days gone by, it is no longer true. In fact, the business press is full of stories of 20-year veterans of companies losing their jobs because they became too expensive. The reality is that you are only as valuable as your current organization thinks you are. If management should change hands—or change views—you could find yourself out of work no matter how impressive your track record is. The problem is that when it comes to leaving organizations most people take a defensive position and try to hold on as long as possible to a job they have outgrown or that has outgrown them. This approach stems from a discomfort with the unknown and an unwillingness to tolerate the ambiguity that inevitably accompanies a job change. If you find yourself strategizing about ways to hang on to a position, it may mean you're resisting the inevitable. If you have trouble identifying what specific contribution you make to the organization, you've already waited too long.

Diagnosis

In a volatile work environment like the corporate America of the 1990s, most jobs have a half-life. A job's half-life, like that of a radioactive mineral, goes through a series of transformations. In its first stage it develops its strength. For a period thereafter it is at its maximum force. Eventually it begins to disintegrate. During the development stage you are learning the ropes by figuring out what's expected of you and how you are going to deliver the goods. Once you've figured things out, you have the opportunity to perform at maximum levels. This period can be very satisfying and rewarding. Eventually, however, your effectiveness will most likely diminish. This may not happen until you're of retirement age, in which case there's no problem. However, if you're like most of the population, it will happen sooner than you expect or are prepared to deal with. Catching yourself early in the diminished capacity curve is key to your recovery.

Prognosis

Once you've reached peak performance and are sure you've done your best in a job, chances are it's time to move on. If your job is still satisfying even though you're no longer functioning at capacity, it's not too late to make a move. If you've waited until things are really bad—what a friend of mine calls the "out the door before you're out the window" syndrome—then your task is much harder, and chances are it will take much longer.

Prescription

To save you from becoming victimized by this condition, the thing to remember is that no job is permanent and that your career—if you are to feel truly secure—is based on your competence, not on your contract. Too many people have sought security in their organization only to find it pulled out from under them by some unforeseen force. Blind faith in organizations or institutions creates a dependency that even the most talented and sought after professionals cannot count on. The best thing you can do for your career is to take control of it during the good times, when you've got the energy and perspective to make sound decisions. That way you'll avoid having to make decisions that tend to yield poor results—decisions made in desperation.

I see this phenomenon often in my Career Renewal workshops. While I draw many clients who are about to lose their jobs, the ones that I find most exciting to work with are those whose jobs are going fine. These people are planning for the future, for when things change and they find themselves looking for work. The contrast between the imminently unemployed and the stable workers is remarkable. Those taking the opportunity to assess their current situation and plan for the future engage in a rich exploration of the possibilities. The result of the process is the development of an exciting, challenging, inspiring plan. Those faced with having to find a new job engage in a struggle characterized by a lack of confidence, a lack of hope, and a sense of powerlessness over their future.

What this means, while it might sound crazy, is that you should be looking for work when work is going well. This does not necessarily mean leaving your organization. If there are opportunities for advancement or change within your organization that make you more valuable to your employer, you should consider those changes. While it's tempting to stay in a position once you've achieved prominence, showing the employer that you've got other things to offer heightens your value. If, however, you find yourself at the top of the heap in your organization and your specialty is such that you have little else to offer, the worst thing you can do is stay in a position that leaves you covering no new territory. Unless you can sustain peak performance in that role, you'll eventually find yourself boxed into a corner and wishing you had made a move when you had the chance.

Here are some ways to test the reality of your situation to find out whether you're in danger of staying too long in a position:

- A sense of boredom as you move through the day, most days.

- A sense that you know everything there is to know about what you do.

- Regular periods of daydreaming about doing something else.

- A feeling that most of what you do is easy for you.

- Many days, it takes you only half your work time to do what needs to be done.

- A feeling of uncertainty about the importance of what you do for the organization.

- A belief that you've already made the biggest contribution you can in your current position.

If you answer yes to any of these statements, there's a good chance that it's time for you to move on. If you don't decide to move on, it's likely that someone else in your organization will soon force you to. It is to your distinct advantage to read the writing on the wall before you're read the riot act and then make a move while you've got the energy and the room to make one that's in your best interest.

WHEN YOU'RE A JACK-OF-ALL-TRADES AND A MASTER OF NONE

Symptoms

This is for those of you who feel you know a little about everything and a lot about nothing. There was a period, not too long ago, when conventional wisdom suggested that everyone be a generalist. This led many people misguidedly to believe that they need not specialize in anything. The problem is that in a technologically advanced society—where access to information has created a level playing field in many disciplines—those left without a specialty run the risk of being valueless. In an age when everyone is screaming about "value-added," this can be quite perplexing. If you cannot demonstrate your value to your organization, you are headed for the outplacement office. If you sense that you are extremely dispensable and others see you as such, you may be getting caught in the generalist trap.

Diagnosis

In considering your range of expertise, you might think of three levels: The first is expert, the second is working knowledge, and the third is dabbling. If you can think of at least three areas in which you consider yourself to be an expert—not necessarily the world's foremost expert, but someone who knows more about that area than most people do—then you've got nothing to fear here. Some people, intimidated by the word "expert," find themselves lacking in this category but have no trouble coming up with three areas in which they have a working knowledge. These people are also relatively safe in that they've got enough of a grasp of several areas and if need be could probably work themselves up to the expert category. The people with the biggest problem are the dabblers, those who embraced the notion of the generalist so fully that they have no expertise and no area over which they can even claim a working knowledge.

If you've been a dabbler, it's time to realize that in the age of the "totalist" you need to be both a generalist *and* a specialist. While having a well-rounded repertoire of generic skills is important, without a specialty you run the risk of being interchangeable with too many other nonspecializing professionals.

Prognosis

The bad news is that lacking a specialty leaves you vulnerable and too easily replaced. The good news is that becoming a specialist is easier than it's ever been. If you're a valued employee to the extent that your organization is willing to invest in you, you can overcome the problem, and there's a good chance you can get your organization to help you do it. If you can find something you're genuinely excited about to warrant specializing and can convince your organization it's in their best interest to help you, there's nothing to stop you from rectifying this problem. Even if you're currently unemployed, if you're willing to spend the time and a little money getting specialized, it will pay off in the long run when you can market yourself as an expert rather than as just another good employee.

Prescription

Get focused. The problem with most generalists is that their focus is too scattered. While others rely on them for support services, the problem with being the generalist is that your support role is often invisible. The experts get the credit, even if you've done a lot of the work. Getting to the point where you know more than anyone else about a particular subject related to your organization's work makes you stand out as an indispensable commodity. Even if your role as a generalist is unchanged within the organization, the fact that you have taken the time to become better than most people in a particular area will set you apart from the crowd and save you when downsizing or reorganizing eliminates the "nonessential" jobs.

LANDING ON YOUR FEET WHEN YOU'VE MADE A BAD MOVE

Symptoms

Nothing is more disconcerting than discovering, after you've engaged in a rigorous search to find the best position, that you've made a bad move and need to start your search all over again. While any job takes time to get used to, if, after four to six months, you come to the conclusion that you're in the wrong position, it's time to act. If you find yourself dreading the beginning of the workday and moving through what seems to be an endless routine as you wait for the clock to strike five, you've probably gotten yourself into a bad situation. If you find yourself fantasizing about what you'd rather be doing or, worse, thinking about how much better the job you left was than the job you're in, you know you've got a problem.

Diagnosis

What's most important here, as with many diagnoses, is accuracy. If in fact you've made a bad move, you need to assess what went wrong accurately so that you are sure to fix the right thing. I know of one man who has established what I believe is a very destructive career pattern—one based on an inaccurate diagnosis of the problem. The man is a hospital administrator who in the past four years has changed jobs eight times! This is the pattern: He gets a job, takes two months to learn the ropes, and spends the next two months doing the job. By the end of the two months, he decides he doesn't like working in "that place." It takes him two more months to find another job. He then repeats the six-month cycle. What's clear to me—and increasingly clear to him as he finds it more difficult to get a position—is that he has mistakenly diagnosed his problem. The problem is not that he keeps ending up in inferior facilities; on the contrary, he's gotten work in some very good places. The real problem is that he no longer finds value in being a hospital administrator. When pressed to discuss it, he clearly no longer finds the problems challenging, the environment stimulating, or the work interesting. His dilemma is much more threatening than simply not liking the place where he works.

Prognosis

As with many progressive diseases, the longer you deny the reality of the problem, the worse things get. The man in the previous story is running the risk of irreparable damage to his career as the result of a pattern of failed positions. Most people with this problem are probably in less damaging situations. Nonetheless, what will make the difference to you in landing on your feet or not is accurately diagnosing what went wrong so that it won't happen again. If you can be honest with yourself and maintain your perspective in what can be a depressing period, you can recover from a mismatch.

Prescription

The first thing you need to do when you find you've made a bad move is to explore your options. Many people caught in the emotional upheaval of realizing they've made a bad choice make the mistake of thinking their new employer is the enemy. Chances are good that unless you've allowed conditions to deteriorate considerably, those who hired you are still invested in your success. Before you decide to leave a new organization, take a close look at what isn't working. If there's a way to change the nature of your position that makes it more palatable, try that first. It may be that the position has been a problem for anyone who's ever held it and that you can save it and yourself at the same time. If you come to the realization that there's no way that you and this position are compatible, explore the possibility of making a move within the organization. Remember, they thought enough of you to hire you above all other applicants. It's safe to assume they still value your potential contribution and would see your leaving as a considerable loss.

If after pursuing these options, you come to the ultimate conclusion that your relationship to the organization is unsalvageable and you need to get out, you must develop a workable strategy that helps you move with finesse. I've seen too many people handle this situation so clumsily that they find themselves embroiled in an elaborate scenario of lies that leaves their self-esteem in tatters. One man I knew, determined to keep his discontent a secret until he found another job, created a mythological family illness to cover his frequent absences from work to conduct interviews with prospective employers. Another man developed an elaborate plan for making discreet phone calls to the point where he would run down the street during breaks to make calls from a phone booth that he believed ensured his privacy. He was shocked one day when a colleague sarcastically said, "Trying out for the Olympics? I didn't know phone calling was now part of the decathlon."

The point is that creating elaborate scenarios to mask your discontent only inflicts more damage to your already fragile ego. Admitting defeat to yourself and to others is a difficult and humbling experience—one that some people like to avoid at all cost. However, concealing your mistake creates an additional layer of trouble over a situation that is already complex enough. My advice on this matter is to bite the bullet and let your employer know that things are not working out. Chances are that your boss already knows and has been trying to figure out a graceful way to get rid of you. Your initiative in the matter will lead to a sense of relief for both of you. More than likely your employer will cooperate in helping you to move on so that you can be replaced with someone more suitable for the job. By being open about the situation, you remove the barriers to finding a better match. You get the room you need to pursue new work honestly and openly. You can stop looking over your shoulder, and can start running for your health rather than out of fear. Most important, you can regain your self-respect in what often can be a very self-defeating time.

Once you get things out in the open, you've positioned yourself to get past the crisis. However, you need to realize that it may be a while before you can make a change. If your employer is willing, see if you can negotiate a reasonable time period to find work (six months to a year is not unreasonable). Be sure your employer knows that you intend to do a competent job during this period and are not merely asking to be carried for an extended period. This will give you the time and freedom to look carefully for your next position.

You need to realize that this can be a very stressful time. You're in transition, recovering from a bad move, and trying to juggle your current responsibilities and a job search at the same time. Make sure you take care of yourself. Many people find this is a good time to seek counseling or therapy to help deal with the emotional implications of the situation. Finding a way to relieve stress through exercise or other leisure activities is also important.

Many people find visualization techniques helpful. Imagine yourself through the transition and beginning your new job, which you are confident is a better match than your current one. If you need an extra lift, imagine yourself moving through your first day on the new job. This will not only boost your energy but also help you guide your search. Finally, don't be too hard on yourself. Many people beat themselves up needlessly over making a bad move. Keep in mind that what happened to you could happen to anyone. The important thing is to get over it and not repeat the mistake.

HANDLING GAPS IN YOUR HISTORY

Symptoms

Finding yourself with a gap of a year or more in your employment history can be difficult when you are marketing yourself to prospective employers. While there are various legitimate reasons for having a gap, the important thing is finding a way to present that gap so that it does not influence your chances negatively.

Diagnosis

The first question is how controversial the gap in history is. If you took time out from work to raise a family, go back to school, or receive specialized training, then all you need do is find the best way to describe what you did, making sure your presentation reflects time well spent. If your gap creates an impression of you that is less than desirable, however, you need a careful strategy for overcoming a potentially negative response.

Some of the trickier situations are those tied to health problems, either physical or mental. Also difficult are those situations that raise doubts about your ambition and level of productivity. For example, I live in an area that has a fairly large American Buddhist community. There are several meditation retreat centers within driving distance. Over the years I've had several clients whose chosen religion is Buddhism. Some of these clients practice their religion by engaging in spiritual retreats in which their primary activity is meditation. These retreats can go on for long periods. In fact, one of my clients spent eight years in meditative retreat. Most of her time was spent on meditation, although after some probing I found out that over the years she had performed tasks essential to the maintenance of the retreat center. The key for her was learning how to present those years in a way that made her prospective employer curious rather than suspicious.

Health problems pose a threat to your employment because they often raise a red flag for the employer, who in most cases will be taking on a signficant amount of the burden of your health care costs. Physical ailments can be a problem if they appear chronic or if the work you're applying for is physically demanding. A history of mental health problems is probably the most complex in that many employers are naive as to the range of conditions and ignorant about the ability of people with mental health problems to lead productive lives.

Prognosis

As in any sensitive area, your success here will be influenced by the extent to which you can present your gap in work history in a way that eases rather than heightens your potential employer's anxiety.

Prescription

This is a tricky area to prescribe for since these issues are, to say the least, sensitive issues. It would be presumptuous of me to think that I could tell anyone faced with these potential barriers what they should do. More than any other situation, these circumstances must be considered individually. Someone faced with a gap in work history resulting from a physical or mental illness or from an extended absence from the work force for personal reasons must decide individually how to handle it. What I can offer are the following perspectives to consider.

Gaps Caused by Personal Life-Style Choices   Absences from the work force for religious or life-style reasons can cause you problems if you try to cover them up or make excuses for them. The best approach is a position of strength, for example: "I took a year off to travel because I wanted to see the world. I was afraid if I waited longer I'd never do it. It was a wonderful year. I learned a lot about cultural differences and feel renewed. I am now ready to settle into a job that taps all my strengths." Consider this response by a long-term Buddhist retreat participant: "Some people have a hard time understanding how someone could spend so much time in meditative retreat. What they don't realize is how meditation can strengthen your spirit and have a positive effect on every part of your life. I can't wait to find a job that's really a good match and dig my teeth into it."

Gaps Caused by Physical Illness Most employers confronted with the prospect of hiring someone who's been out of the work force because of a physical illness want reassurance that the illness has passed and the person has fully recovered. While your health history is no potential employer's business— unless it limits your performance—you can be sure that those doing the hiring will be concerned and may choose someone else if they haven't been satisfied that you're not a risk.

Presenting yourself as a healthy, vibrant individual can go a long way in easing their anxiety. If you've had a serious illness, you may or may not want to divulge that information. Regardless of what you choose to say, it's probably best to wait until you're well into the selection process. Once they really want you, they're unlikely to reject you because you've had some health problems in the past.

Gaps Caused by Mental Illness Even though there's been a wellspring of popular press on mental illness, it's amazing how ignorant most people still are. Chances are if you have had a bout with mental illness or have a chronic problem, you are going to have a difficult time getting an employer to see beyond that. If you've been hospitalized with a mental disorder, your situation is all the more delicate. The reality is that in this day and age many people recover from mental illness, and many others find ways to control it to the point where they lead stable, productive lives. Unfortunately, fear around mental illness is such that knowledge of your condition by prospective employers can cause you, more often than not, to lose opportunities.

I learned a great deal about how to handle such a situation from a client of mine who was hospitalized three years for severe depression. The client came to me after experiencing difficulty in finding a job. He was a certified public accountant who wanted to get back into accounting. His initial approach to the job market was to deal with prospective employers honestly and openly, sharing his past accounting experience with them and filling them in on his recent hospitalization. After several encounters with amiable recruiters who tactfully said no, my client decided to try a different tack. His hunch was that his recent hospitalization—not his successful track record with a big six accounting firm—was preventing him from getting offers. He decided that he needed to present the past three years of his life in a different light. While in the hospital he participated actively in its occupational therapy program and became a proficient ceramist. Upon leaving the hospital, he had gotten a job as a waiter just to tide him over until he could find some accounting work. To present himself to prospective employers in a new way, he began telling them that for the past three years he had been studying ceramics and had also most recently been working as a waiter to make ends meet. He told them he had recently decided to stop pursuing ceramics and wanted to get back into accounting. He knew that some employers would not respect his artistic diversion, so he started pursuing work in places he suspected would be more open to his divergent interests. Eventually he got a job as an accountant in a large wholesale natural foods distributorship. After a while he gave them a more complete picture of his background.

Now some of you might say that my client got his job by lying. He would disagree. He would tell you that he decided to share his background with prospective employers in a selective way that would not hurt his chances at employment. He would also tell you that after a few months he told the people he worked with about his entire history. While some of them were surprised, they all understood why he hadn't told them before. More important, now that they know him, it has absolutely no impact on their working relationship.

While these examples may seem like more extreme reasons for gaps in employment history than you are likely to have, my intention is to show you that even in the most difficult circumstances there are ways to manage the problem. Most likely any personal gaps you have are not as challenging. The greatest lesson to be learned here for handling gaps in employment history comes from the accountant-ceramist. He was not afraid to adapt his presentation of himself to free him from any constraints his history might create. He did not lie. He merely chose to tell the truth in a way that was not damaging to his prospects. If you have a difficult past to contend with and you allow an interview to become an inquisition, you are forced to divulge information that, shared prematurely, can work against you. If you can fashion a personal presentation that accurately but safely conveys your history, you've managed to overcome the potential obstacles that gaps in history can create. Remember, potential employers don't have to love you—or know everything about you. They just need to be convinced that you can do the job.

THE DANGER OF LETTING SOMEONE ELSE HANDLE YOUR CAREER

Symptoms

A gnawing feeling that things are getting out of your control and that someone else is making the important decisions for

you means it's time to pay attention. Many people make their living off the talent of other people. If you find yourself being managed by someone else and you don't like the way things are going, you had better do something to regain control.

Diagnosis

Handlers are people whose work involves making other people successful. Examples of high-level handlers are people like publicists, agents, public relations specialists, and image consultants.

Most people are not likely to find themselves being "handled" by such people. However, as the career marketplace gets more complex and more competitive, increasing numbers of people will find themselves relying on handlers. You might find yourself "being handled" by an executive or management recruiter or an employment agent. If you've been let go recently, it's entirely possible that you could find yourself in the hands of an outplacement consultant. If you've been frustrated in your job search, you may have even solicited the help of a professional career consultant.

Each of these resources can prove to be a tremendous asset to you in your career management. Problems emerge, however, around priorities. For many of these handlers time is money. The sooner they help you find a new job, the sooner they can collect their fee and move on to new clients. For them, time is of the essence. For you, quality should be of the essence. This could mean that you find yourself pressured to accept a position you don't really want. If you're not feeling good about your relationship with your handler or are uncomfortable about the nature of the opportunities coming your way, it's time to reassess the relationship.

Prognosis

This is what a friend of mine calls a high-class problem. If you're fortunate enough to have someone working on your behalf, you will most likely benefit from the relationship. All you need do is remember that you are in charge and that this person's role is to help you get what you want. As long as you aren't desperate and are prepared to assert yourself, you shouldn't have any problem making it clear to the handlers what it is you want and don't want.

Prescription

The sooner you establish the ground rules for the relationship, the better. Some handlers will sweep you off your feet with promises of wealth and prosperity that all your better judgment falls aside. The best thing to do is to let this person know early in the relationship that you are very concerned about not only finding a job, but also finding the best possible job for you right now, given your background and goals. What most handlers do is try to place you in a job that is as similar to what you've been doing as possible. Career changers make most handlers very nervous because they assume your search will take much longer. If you're not looking to change careers, all you need do is point out in no uncertain terms what the parameters are for you in terms of new work. If you want to explore the possibility of changing fields, be prepared for some resistance. Handlers will tell you that changing careers is very difficult and advise against it. If they won't cooperate and help you to explore alternatives, you need to consider dropping them and finding someone else. Chances are, if one handler found you worth working with, others will as well. Find someone who is a good listener and willing to follow your lead. If you don't, you may end up following their lead right into the wrong job.

An Inside Look at Outplacement   As recently as five years ago, you would have been unlikely to find yourself in the hands of an outplacement consultant unless you were an upper-level executive. The field of outplacement is in its infancy—about 20 years old by most accounts. Yet today, it is a multibillion dollar industry. Outplacement services are increasingly available to a broad range of workers, including middle managers, line workers, and in some organizations anyone who is being "let go." Because of rapid growth and change in the industry, it can be difficult to know what to expect from an outplacement outfit. Services range anywhere from access to a phone and copier to complex psychological testing and network building. Some outplacement firms are multimillion dollar operations with offices in every major city; others are small one-site businesses with a few career consultants.

Knowing what to expect and what to ask for can make a real difference in your being able to benefit from whatever outplacement services are available to you. When it comes to outplacement firms, big is not necessarily better. While I was preparing a speech to deliver at the national meeting of the Association of Outplacement Consulting Firms, I did some research on the subject. After talking to many people who had received outplacement assistance, I found a mix of reviews. Some people who had been through a large "outplacement process" run by one of the big firms felt as though they had been part of a herd being put through the paces. Others felt they had been subject to entirely too much psychological testing. "I didn't need therapy," said one bank executive. "I needed a new job." What this man was referring to was a battery of tests that some firms have begun to give to all their clients as a rule of thumb. He wanted to stay in his field and find another position similar to his old one, and was frustrated by what he felt was an overcomplication of a straightforward process.

In my speech at the outplacement conference, I suggested that firms needed to reassess their approach and develop ways to assess individual needs before running every client through what was beginning to sound like a cookie-cutter process. As I spoke, I saw many heads nodding in agreement. I went on to say that it seemed to me that outplacement, like any young industry trying to establish itself, might be suffering from growing pains that are producing an overbureaucratization of their own methods. I suggested that any new industry struggling to establish itself runs the risk of becoming self-serving and creating an unnecessary infrasturcture to support its growth. Again, I saw many heads nodding. At the end of the speech, numerous outplacement consultants confirmed that my observations were on target. Six months later, I was still receiving letters and phone calls from people who've listened to the tape of the speech and said my comments were right on the mark.

The point of all this is that if you find yourself in the hands of an outplacement consulting firm be aware of the danger of getting swept into a process that may not be what you really need. Be sure to assert yourself and let them know your needs. If all you want is resume assistance, don't get caught up in taking a battery of tests. If you want to change careers, don't allow yourself to be pushed into a position similar to your old one. If you need psychological support, see if they can provide it from a qualified source. Whatever you do, remember that they've been retained by your employer to help you, not to meet their quotas.

Often you won't be able to choose which firm you work with. If you can, carefully examine what each has to offer. A large firm may have a better network to tap into and access to better resources; a small firm might be able to provide more personalized service. Choose the one that can best respond to your needs. Incidentally, if you're being let go and no outplacement services have been offered, ask your employer to foot the bill for such a service. They may very well agree, and you'll find yourself with some invaluable support that can make your search efforts much easier.

SELLING YOURSELF SHORT BECAUSE YOU'RE CHANGING FIELDS

Symptoms

A relatively recent widespread phenomenon is the large number of people in the work force who shift from one arena to another. As the baby boom generation matures, career change will likely become as matter of fact as the dual-career family. Nevertheless, the majority of people who decide to shift fields develop a sense of insecurity about their marketability in a new field. Many career changers feel that if they had chosen right the first time they wouldn't be in this position. Consequently, many of them feel like the new kid on the block, someone who needs to apologize for lack of familiarity with the field. This uneasiness can have a dramatic impact on how they present themselves, on the offers they get, and on their ability to negotiate effectively. If you find yourself lowering your expectations because you're changing fields, there's a good chance you are falling into this trap.

Diagnosis

The severity of this condition has to do with the depth of your psychological insecurity and the extent to which that insecurity manifests itself in your interactions with contacts in the new field and prospective employers. If you find yourself saying, "I really don't know anything about your field, but think I might like to pursue it," "I know I don't have any real experience in your area," or "I understand that being new to the field I'd have to start at the bottom and work my way up," then you're well on your way to selling yourself short. While it's natural to feel uncomfortable in a new arena, the last thing you want to project to a prospective employer or even to contacts in a new field is that you come cheap.

Prognosis

Here's where perspective comes in. If you can realize and remember that you have a successful track record, then you have a good chance to overcome selling yourself short. People who overcome this obstacle are aware that in most jobs what makes them successful is their ability to grasp new ideas, analyze problems, formulate solutions, and implement those solutions. Regardless of what field you're in, if you can master a new discipline quickly and apply your critical thinking skills to the problem, you can succeed in just about any field. The key here is knowing your core skills and marketing them—not your knowledge of a particular topic. If you can do that, there's nothing to stop you from breaking into any field you want—at a top salary.

Prescription

In this information age, access to knowledge is at everyone's fingertips. What separates people is what they can do with that information. If you sold automobiles, you can sell encyclopedias. If you taught high school students, you can train managers. If you managed a supermarket, you can manage an insurance office. The important thing to realize in shifting fields is that what you are selling are your skills, not your knowledge of a new arena. Knowledge can be gained much faster than skill can be developed.

If you're smart, you'll find a niche in your new area of interest that capitalizes on what you do well. Once you find that niche, there's no reason to sell yourself short. Market yourself as someone who has what it takes to do the job well. If an employer says, "Well, we'll have to start you low because you're new to the field," you can respond, "I may have a little to learn about this product, but my depth of experience in delivering quality products in the past shows that I've got what it takes to do this job well. I expect to perform at top levels for you, and I expect to be compensated at that level. If I didn't think I could do this job well, I wouldn't be here." If that's not enough to get you toward the top of their salary scale, you can also add, "Besides, coming out of the field I've just been in gives me an added advantage over those people just starting out. I can bring experience and a track record to this job that makes me worth at least as much as the competition."

What you do by taking this sort of tack (use your own

words) is turn the table on the interviewer who is using the common negotiating ploy of making you feel that what you have to offer them is of less value than what they have to offer you. Preparation for this sort of psychological jousting will make the difference between entering a position as a respected professional (with the appropriate benefits and salary) and entering as a newcomer who's been given a break—and a very different set of benefits and salary. The choice is yours.

WHEN YOU MAKE A BAD FIRST IMPRESSION

Symptoms

Many observers of human behavior agree that first impressions carry a great deal of weight when it comes to people's assessments of each other. This is unfortunate since we all know that there are times when, for a variety of reasons, we don't put our best feet forward in first encounters. You know you've got this problem when you walk away from a first encounter with a prospective employer—or an important client or customer—and know that, for whatever reason, you've blown it.

From Potato Chips to Chalk Dust   I'd like to tell you about a bad impression I made a long time ago and how I managed to turn it around. It is, like most bad first impression stories, a little embarrassing. I had been working as an English teacher when I decided teaching wasn't for me. I took a short hiatus for a job delivering potato chips. While in this job, I decided I wanted to try teaching again, this time at a different level and in a different setting. I had gotten a call to interview for a high school teaching job in a prestigious school system. I was on my way home from delivering potato chips to change into my interview suit when my truck had a flat tire. I quickly changed the flat and then realized I had a choice to make—either be late for the interview or go directly to it without changing clothes. I decided that lateness would be a worse offense than walking into the principal's office in my potato chip delivery uniform, complete with the Wise Owl embossed on my shirt pocket. As I extended my tire-greased hand to the principal (whose office and dress were immaculate), I noticed him wincing twice, first at my greasy hand and second at seeing the owl on my shirt.

In an effort to break the ice, I commented on my unfortunate mishap and on how I wouldn't come to work in my uniform if I were hired. Although the conversation went well, I could tell by his nonverbal behavior that all he saw when he looked at me was a greasy owl. Toward the end of the interview, he let me know that he was desperate for a teacher—my first ray of hope. He needed someone to start the following Monday. I told him that I was very interested but was scheduled for minor surgery that Monday (his third surprise) and couldn't possibly start until the following Monday. He told me that the delay was unacceptable and that he enjoyed meeting me (which I knew wasn't true).

On my way home, I felt disappointed. Here was a good opportunity to get into a very prestigious system at a time when they needed someone and I had blown it with a bad first impression. I remember wondering what I could do to turn it around. What I came up with has become a rule of thumb for me. When a person makes a bad first impression, the only way to overcome it is to make an outstanding second impression. When I got home, I called my physician and asked him if we could reschedule my surgery for Christmas break. He said there'd be no problem. I called the principal and told him I thought the job was a perfect match for me, so much so that I had canceled my hospitalization in order to start Monday if he wanted me to. He was so aghast at my willingness to, as he put it, "rearrange my life to accommodate him" that he offered me the job on the spot.

Diagnosis

Diagnosing this problem is simple. When you've made a bad first impression, you usually know it. While your experience may not be as vivid as the potato chip incident, a feeling of regret or remorse over having said or done something that was ill received in a first encounter means that you need to consider ways to undo your gaffe.

Prognosis

The worst thing you can do about a bad first impression is pretend it didn't happen. Many people, feeling embarrassed or frustrated at their inability to wind back the clock and do it over, choose to act as if such an incident never occurred. The problem with this reaction is that first impressions are so powerful that the receiver of your blunder probably hasn't forgotten. Without action on your part, that first impression remains the dominant impression of you. People are often impressed with those who can admit their shortcomings or mistakes. If you're willing to show some humility and can come back with an outstanding second impression, you should be able to undo the damage.

Prescription

Don't just sit there wallowing in regret. Respond in an honest, self-revealing, yet positive way, and chances are you can overcome any poor showing. Letting someone know you said or did something you feel bad about will take them by surprise. Most people are not used to hearing such candor. If you did something in a first enounter that you truly regret, such as making a comment that was in bad taste, own up to your error in judgment. Often a willingness to come forward is enough to adjust someone's impression. If what you did was merely use naive poor judgment, like bringing an owl to the interview, then do something that impresses the other person so much that the initial contact is overshadowed. Hard as it may be to swallow your pride, admitting that you've done something that needs undoing is the best way to turn a potential loss into a potential opportunity.

WHEN YOUR JOB IS INTERFERING WITH YOUR CAREER

Symptoms

This seeming contradiction occurs when you allow yourself the luxury of letting your job control your career. It happens all the time. In fact, many of the people I see as clients come to me because at age 40 or 50 they are experiencing, for the first time in their lives, a situation in which their job is not taking their career where they want it to go. Some people never have this problem and are fortunate enough to have their jobs provide them with the kind of career they're looking for. If what you are doing for work feels less and less like what you want to be doing, you may be suffering from this malady.

Diagnosis

Ideally, your job exists in the context of a career path: What you are doing is preparing you for what you want to do next; if you keep on track, eventually you will get to where you want to be. Unfortunately, this is not always the case; if we believe the statistics, it is increasingly less the case.

The problem can exist in two ways. If you hate what you do, it's pretty clear that it's time for a change. People who hate their jobs don't perform well, and they owe it to themselves and to their employers to get out. If you are one of these people, you know it, and we need not dwell on the fact that you need to make a change. Far more difficult is the situation in which you like your job but feel it's not moving you in the right direction. This is difficult to face because if you have what most people consider "a good job," you will no doubt feel societal pressure to keep it. Messages like "You don't know how lucky you are," "You should be glad you have a good job with a good company," and "This is a tough time to make a change" can serve to keep you in your career-damaging job. You might hear these messages from your spouse, parents, children, colleagues, bosses, or your own psyche. Many people have a difficult time understanding why anyone would give up a good job. The reality is that one person's dream job is another person's nightmare.

One woman I know is a very successful school administrator. She's been principal of a private school and held a variety of highly respected positions in secondary and higher education. She's also a healer and stress management trainer. In fact, she's developed a program for working with chronically overweight people that I believe could revolutionize the weight-loss industry. Her problem is that she doesn't have the time to develop and market her program. In a recent conversation she told me she had just resigned from her administrative job at a community college. She's decided to put all her energy into developing her private stress management and weight-control programs. When I asked her why she made the shift, she replied simply, "I knew I wasn't doing what I was supposed to be doing. This is what I should be doing." When probed further, she made it clear that she knew she was a good administrator but also knew that she couldn't care less about all the things administrators need to care about. Her heart and mind were focused on her work in managing stress and life-style adjustment. Even though she left the security of a successful position doing something she did well, she was convinced that the job was interfering with her career path and her desire to do something that really matters to her.

Prognosis

Facing up to the reality that your job—and your success—has led you to dissatisfaction is difficult. From childhood we are led to believe that if we do well in our chosen path, we will achieve success and happiness. It is a rude awakening to realize that the two don't necessarily go hand in hand. In fact, the greater the investment we have in our success, the more difficult it is to admit to its shortcomings and make a change. I see this most often with highly specialized fields like medicine and law.

When practitioners I meet find out that I am a career consultant, what often follows is a confession that they feel bored, overburdened, or both by what they do. What follows almost immediately is, "But what am I going to do, throw it all away?" Indeed, it would be difficult to imagine a physician or attorney giving up a privileged profession after having paid so dearly to attain that status. How unfortunate, however, for the person stuck in a profession they don't want for the rest of their lives! The only way to get past the obstacles placed on you by your success is willingly and openly facing the fact that this success may no longer hold the allure it once held. Only then can you be free to move on to your next career.

Prescription

The best way to get a handle on the real problem is to concentrate on your day-to-day routine. Focusing on the big picture only distorts your view by seducing you with the trappings, status, profits, or illusion of what it's like to be in your profession. I've known countless consultants drawn to the field by the allure of romantic travel to distant places for the purpose of influencing high-level executives toward achieving high-minded goals. Many of them hang up their briefcases after relentless flights, dreary hotel rooms, and the constant pressure of putting out fires in crippled organizations. While some consultants find ways to create the kind of life they want, far too many are left disappointed because they didn't pay attention to the reality of the job—the day-to-day activities. They got too caught up in the illusion of the glamour of consulting.

With this problem, the best way to sort reality from fantasy is to focus on the extent to which what you do every day satisfies your current needs and future goals. Once the adminstrator turned stress management trainer realized that her daily activities held little relevance for her given how she wanted to spend her time and what she wanted to accomplish, her choice became clear. If you want to be sure your job is not interfering with your career, take a moment and think about what you did at work today and whether it was satisfying your current needs and moving you toward your career goals. If it wasn't, you'd better reassess your situation or you might find yourself, like the consultants I mentioned, hating the reality of the work you thought you'd love.

IF YOU'VE BEEN FIRED

Symptoms

The pink slip. Seriously, we've all heard the horror stories about people arriving at work to find their offices no longer exist, or being called to the front office and then escorted back to their work stations to pick up their things and leave the premises immediately. Nothing is more disruptive to your career than finding yourself involuntarily without work, yet much can be done to minimize the damage to your career.

Diagnosis

While being fired carries a certain stigma, the circumstances surrounding your dismissal and, more important, your responses to the situation will greatly influence your ability to get back on your feet and leave this unfortunate incident behind. The first thing to consider is the nature of the dismissal. Were you let go as part of a group that was being laid off, were you the target of a downsizing that had little to do with your performance, or were you terminated because of some activity or lack of activity on your part? Also important is gaining an understanding of the progression leading to your dismissal. Was it something you could have or should have anticipated, or did it come as a total shock?

We are all uncomfortable with the process of people losing their jobs. If you doubt this, consider the number and range of euphemisms for the word "fired." They include but are not limited to laid off, let go, canned, terminated, outplaced, and outcounseled, to name a few. Just as those doing the firing feel a need to use different words to describe different firings, you need to take a careful look at the circumstances surrounding your termination and develop ways of reconciling the event to yourself and then of presenting it to prospective employers. Understanding the circumstances of your firing can help you figure out a strategy for leaving your organization under the best conditions and for approaching new organizations in the least vulnerable way.

One of the more difficult problems to overcome with the loss of your job is often the accompanying loss of your identity. Americans identify themselves with their work. Think about it. When you meet someone new, what's the first thing you ask? "What do you do for a living?" People who have been fired often experience a crisis of confidence caused by the elimination of a key aspect of their identities. Such a loss can leave you depressed and lacking in energy—the opposite of what you need. Before moving into action, you need to come to terms with this loss and find a way to cope with the difficult times ahead.

Prognosis

In the age of downsizing, being fired is a lot less damaging than it used to be. The stigma, while still a problem, is much less now than in the days when losing your job was synonymous with gross incompetence. On any given day, large numbers of competent, talented people lose their jobs as the result of corporate shake-ups and reorganizations. Expectations are such that even those who lose jobs because of incompetence can find a way to salvage their reputations and move on to better opportunities. If you can come to terms with the loss and find a way of presenting yourself to prospective employers that de-emphasizes your exit from your last organization and emphasizes your accomplishments within it, you're on your way to surviving what is undoubtedly one of the more stressful life experiences.

Prescription

Like being asked for a divorce, being fired is something you're never really prepared for. However, there may be warning signals. If you suspect you're about to be fired, the worst thing to do is to wait for the ax to fall. If you want to keep your job, the best thing to do is to approach your boss with your concern and see if there's any way you can salvage the situation. If there isn't, one alternative before you're terminated is to arrange for your departure. The old line, "You can't fire me, I quit" holds some wisdom here. It is far easier to explain to a prospective employer why you left a position than it is to explain why you were fired. In fact, there are times when you can even use this to your advantage once you've been fired. Many people in this situation ask that they be allowed to resign and often find the employer willing to oblige them. One consideration to keep in mind is that choosing resignation over termination may lead to loss of unemployment benefits. Be sure to consider your needs and priorities before offering to turn a firing into a resignation.

Once the termination has occurred, it makes sense to leave the organization as soon as possible. Many organizations are increasingly thinking this way and urge or direct terminated employees to leave immediately. While this may feel too abrupt, it makes sense for you to comply, given the potential for emotional responses to the event that you might regret later.

Once the termination is official, you need to regroup. This involves several activities. First and perhaps most important is attending to your psychological well being. As I mentioned earlier, the loss of a job can cause devastation to your sense of identity. Find a family member, a friend, or a professional who can help you handle the flood of emotions that will undoubtedly overwhelm you in the first few weeks following the job loss.

Once you've established yourself on solid emotional ground, consider carefully your new relationship with your previous employer. You need several things from them. First, you need some letters of recommendation. This is important because prospective employers will want to see that you had a decent track record prior to your dismissal. More important, you need a sense of good faith with your former employer. This can be tricky if your leaving was not amicable; however, it's essential that you patch things up. More employers are now suspicious about written references and do their reference checks over the phone. Painful as it might be, you should make every effort to talk with the person who was your immediate supervisor and the person he or she reports to. You may find many of these people surprisingly willing to speak with you, even if there's been some bad feeling. The reason is that many organizations find they can learn a lot about their problems from people who are leaving. Exit interviews, in which staff probe those leaving the organization about their thoughts as to the organization's problems, are becoming increasingly popular. They are the perfect opportunity to patch up any bad feelings that might have occurred during or prior to a termination. In most cases, you'll find even the most difficult former bosses eager to bury the hatchet. Most people—there are exceptions—like to end relationships amicably even if their history was a difficult one. Most important, if your last enounter is a positive one, there's a good chance that the referrals you get from this person in the future will be more positive.

Once your emotional state is intact and you've done all you can with your previous employer, it's time to focus your attention on presenting yourself and this blemish on your record to prospective employers. Some people try to hide the fact that they've been fired. I think this is a mistake. First of all it's difficult to present yourself as a strong, positive person if you're fearful of your lie being found out. In addition, it's more than likely that if you've been fired a reference check will uncover the truth and you will lose all your credibility. The best thing to do is to put it on the table early so it doesn't linger in your prospective employer's mind. Don't dwell on it—get it out and move on as quickly as possible. Be sure to use the least damaging language possible. If you convinced your previous employer to let you resign, be sure you communicate that you left by choice. If you were fired, pull out the bag of euphemisms and say you were laid off or let go. If your dismissal occurred as part of a group, let that be known: "I was part of the firm's December layoff." Whatever you say, be sure to say it in as matter-of-fact a way as possible, indicating that this is something that just happened and is not in any way a reflection of your competence. Never say anything bad about the previous employer. While it might be tempting, you'll only box yourself into a corner and be seen as a vindictive malcontent. Once you've said you were fired, quickly move on to other territory and cover, if you can, a review of your greatest accomplishments in the last job and in previous ones.

Most important, remember that none of this is easy. There will undoubtedly be some people who will hold your being fired against you, and there's nothing you can do about it. However, there will also be people who appreciate that everyone goes through tough times and will not hold this against you. Finally, keep in mind that losing your job does not mean losing your career. This experience will diminish in importance over time. Remember, you can bounce back—people do it every day. With careful planning and careful attention to all the factors I've talked about, you can make it through this difficult experience and find yourself back on track.

THREE

Organizational Changes that Can Endanger Your Career

Organizational change is inevitable. For companies to survive and thrive in the 1990s and beyond, they must embrace the notion of change. If you find yourself working in an organization that is resistant to change or refuses to change, you'd better think seriously about getting out. Any organization not prepared to adapt to rapid market shifts will find itself out of business or at least at the bottom of its industry.

While the ability and willingness to change and adapt is a critical factor for the successful company, the impact of such a philosophy on individual career management is just as profound. Unless you pay careful attention to how your organization is changing, you may find yourself suddenly faced with the reality that your company no longer has a place for you or that the place they have for you is not where you want to be.

THE PICTURE OF HEALTH: ORGANIZATIONAL WELLNESS

When speaking of organizational wellness here, I am speaking of the organization in relation to you and your career. While many things can happen to an organization that influence its overall wellness, the important thing for you is to determine the impact of those changes on your future. Almost any major—and sometimes minor—organizational change can have a major impact on your career. The organizationally well career manager pays attention to every aspect of organizational change. Technological changes, structural changes, symbolic changes, political changes, cultural changes, and, perhaps most important, human resource changes can all influence your career wellness within the organization.

When an organization introduces a new technology, it can have a broad impact on the people who work there. Some new technologies render certain organizational roles obsolete. Some create the need for new organizational roles. Most important, the introduction of a new technology often creates new performance demands on all the people in the organization. Understanding the impact of a technological change on the way the organization and its employees work will prevent you from becoming a casualty of that new technology.

Reorganizations, restructuring, and downsizing can create challenges to your career ranging from having to deal with a new boss to finding yourself one of the outplaced. It is important to pay attention to structural changes even if you are not directly affected by them since there's a good chance of at least a ripple effect on the way you do your job—and your potential for success within the organization.

Perhaps the most illusive changes you must pay attention to are the symbolic ones. When a company changes its vision or mission statement, goals and objectives, or the images it uses to portray itself, the primary thrust of the organization is shifting. Depending on the nature of the shift, your role could be strengthened or weakened. Your task in the situation is to assess the shift and its potential to help or hinder your career.

Political changes such as mergers, acquisitions, or otherwise informal alliances between your organization and other organizations, as well as changes in the way ownership, management, and employees interact, are cause for significant scrutiny. Employee stock ownership plans can be a real boon to your career if the shift leads to a greater stake in the organization along with greater profits. They can be problematic if you were one of the powerful before and find yourself disenfranchised by the change. With any major shift in control of the organization, there are winners and losers. Paying close attention to these shifts in power and assessing whether the outcomes result in a loss or win for you personally—regardless of the benefits or liabilities for the organization—are key to your career wellness.

Whether or not you are aware of it, the organization you work for has a distinct culture that differentiates it from all other organizations. This culture is unique in its organizational rituals, norms, patterns, and rules. When any of these factors change, the nature of your relationship to the organization changes with it. Paying attention to the subtle and overt changes your organization's culture goes through can help you avoid finding yourself a stranger in a strange land.

Human resource changes are probably the most direct threats to your career. Changes in who reports to whom, who works together, and who has upward access play an important role in your career management. When your formal and informal relationships in an organization change, your ability to do your job and to achieve success are influenced dramatically. Assessing the impact of human resource changes can alert you to problems before they develop and help you plan a course of action, should the changes leave you in a weakened position.

While this may seem overwhelming when all you really want is to do a good job and be appropriately rewarded, it's important to remember that organizational systems are human systems and are therefore complex. Without careful attention to all of these areas, your career wellness will be jeopardized by organizational changes that can endanger your career. This chapter shows you ways to prepare for and handle the potentially most damaging organizational changes.

WHEN A REORGANIZATION LEAVES YOU OUTSIDE THE INNER CIRCLE

Symptoms

Whether you're at the top of your organization, at a middle level, or just starting out, in order to succeed you need access to the people at your level who matter to the organization. Too many people think only of moving up, when what's equally important is that you move in as well. Moving in here means that you are accepted by those in your particular area who are considered important. It's easy to tell when you're part of the inner circle. You feel that you belong, that you're protected, and that the organization will do all it can to help you do your job.

Reorganizations are, by their very nature, disorienting. It can be difficult to determine whether a juggling of roles and relationships has left you an outsider. Finding yourself insecure about your ability to do your job is a warning sign. Finding that access to key organizational players has become more difficult for you is another sign. One of the strongest warning signals is finding that someone who previously had less access and responsibility than you now has more to do and more resources to do it. If you can quickly look around and see others who are in better shape than they were while you feel in considerably worse shape, there's a good chance you've just been booted from the inner circle.

Diagnosis

You should not underestimate the potential damage this can have on your career. Too many people, when faced with this scenario, cling to their title and insist that they haven't lost ground. Titles can be important, but when it comes to assessing the impact of a reorganization they are far less important than an accurate assessment of damages incurred. If you're not careful, you could find yourself vice president for outplacement—your own. The true impact of structural changes such as a reorganization can be better understood by looking at the actual changes, not just the symbolic ones. In order to avoid panic in a reorganization, companies will often avoid changing formal variables like titles, but will make sweeping changes in who reports to whom, who works together and who has upward access that are potentially far more damaging than merely losing one's stripes.

Whenever you find yourself involved in a reorganization—whether it's formal or informal—you need to pay attention to the subtle and not-so-subtle changes that accompany that reshuffling.

Prognosis

Unless your CEO is the type who likes change for the sake of change (how often does the office furniture get rearranged?), there's a good chance that a reorganization is a sign that the organization is in some sort of trouble. There are two kinds of trouble that are cause for alarm: either your department or unit is seen as the source of the problem or your department or unit is seen as a potential solution to the problem. If you suspect your unit is considered the source, then the reorganization is just the tip of the iceberg. You had better figure out a way to turn things around or prepare for your exit interview. If your unit is not considered part of the problem but is seen as a potential solution—that is, if we can cut corners here, we can cut our losses there—then your task is to figure out if you can survive and thrive in the new configuration. Either way, surviving a reorganization is manageable, provided you can give the organization what it needs. The trick is accurately figuring out what problems the reorganization reflects.

Prescription

Most organizational theorists agree that in these volatile times job security has little to do with formal contracts between individuals and organizations and a lot to do with informal connections among key people in the organization. While formal arrangements may protect you in the short run, informal relationships save your neck over the long haul. This means paying very careful attention to your place in the inner circle. You need to have either access to the people at the top or strong connections with those who do have access. If you find your access diminishing, do what you can to salvage it. The best time to deal with the threats that accompany a reorganization is while the reorganization is actually progressing.

Organizational theorist Kurt Lewin described a three-phase process that organizations go through during a change effort. The first phase is unfreezing, when the old ways are dismissed and abandoned. The second phase is changing, when the new ways are molded. The third phase is refreezing, when the new ways are adopted and solidified. The thing to remember is that once refreezing has occurred, it becomes very difficult to undo the change. If you find that what's happening in the course of a reorganization is creating a threat to your career and jeopardizing your position in the inner circle, you had better do something about it while the organization is in the second phase and open to modifications.

For example, say your organization is about to reorganize and you perceive that the changes might hurt your department and make your work more difficult to do or less important to the organization. You could decide, as many people do, to wait until the dust settles before you make your concerns known. The problem with waiting is that once the dust settles and refreezing occurs, your chances of being heard are negligible. The time to voice your concerns is while the dust is flying. At that point everyone's trying to figure out what the refreezing should look like. If you've been part of the inner circle and have access to decision makers, it's likely that you will get heard and avoid irreparable damage to your unit. If it seems inevitable that your work unit is going to be hit hard, it may be time for you to shift within the organization. Now is the time to use your access to the inner circle to make sure you stay in it. Trying to make a move after the reorganization has settled is much harder than doing it when everything else in the organization is also in flux.

What matters here is not that you continue to do the things you've always done the way you've always done them. If you want to continue to play an important role in this organization, you must figure out how you need to change in order to match the changes the organization is experiencing. Figure out how the organization's changes affect your work, adjust your work to match the new needs of the organization, let those in power know what you're doing—and enlist their help in doing it— and your position in the inner circle will be secure.

ASSESSING THE CAREER IMPACT OF A NEW BOSS

Symptoms

If you're any good at managing your career, you know that one of the most important—perhaps the most important—relationships you have on the job is with your boss. Without a solid connection to the person you report to, you are extremely vulnerable. Your boss should be your ally, your protector, your promoter, and ideally your friend. If you've ever had a boss who is all these things, you know what a difference it can make in your willingness and ability to do your job. If you've ever worked for a boss you didn't get along with, you know how tremendously draining and frustrating it can be. If you're smart and lucky, you've developed a relationship with your boss that provides you with support, guidance, advocacy, and a sense of camaraderie.

Unfortunately, no relationship lasts forever, and it's entirely possible that you will stay in a job longer than your boss stays in place, thus giving you the opportunity and challenge of forging a new relationship with a new person.

Diagnosis

The first thing to realize once a change in bosses occurs is that the rules have changed as well. All the assumptions you've made about how you do your work are up for grabs, subject to the impresssions, opinions, and, yes, whims of the new person in charge. If you're lucky, your new leader respects your ways of working and is not interested in remolding you to match his or her style. The most important gauge for determining how difficult new bosses will be is to determine what their priorities are. Are they interested in finding out what you do well and supporting your efforts, or are they interested in putting their stamp on everyone who reports to them?

Prognosis

Anytime you get a new boss, things will be shaky for a while, but finding that your new boss is interested in what you do right as well as what you do differently is a good sign. If the person hired to be your new overseer is secure and confident, there's a good chance your boss's ego won't get in your way and that all you need do is develop rapport and mutual understanding. Once you get to know each other, you can breathe more easily and get back to doing the good work you've been doing.

If your new boss is determined to reshape the work unit to fit his or her style, however, you're probably in for some rough seas. If you've been ready for a change, you may welcome this sort of shake-up; if you felt that things were going well before your previous boss departed, you may find it very difficult to shift gears. You have two choices here. If you're open to change, this could be an opportunity to make some adjustments to your work and forge a strong relationship with your new superior. If you're resistant to change, you may find yourself with little choice but to move on to another position and find another boss who is more compatible.

Regardless of your new boss's style, it's important to remember that a change in command will be unsettling at best and will require some careful observation on your part before you really know whether or not you will survive and thrive with the change.

Prescription

Early on your new boss's style will tell you a great deal about his or her agenda. Someone who initially spends a lot of time listening is probably less driven to mold and control you than someone who starts off by telling you how they think things should work. Someone who shows signs of being a team player rather than an autocrat will also be less likely to insist that you change the way you operate. Sometimes little things like saying "we" versus "I" can clue you in on this new person's need to control.

To make the most of the situation, you need to put yourself in your new boss's shoes. Realize that someone in this position is most likely trying to get a picture of the new team. Who are the strong links and who are the weak? Who are the people most likely to help them succeed, and who are the ones likely to cause them trouble? Your first task—should you decide you want to work for this person—is to form a personal alliance, a one-to-one connection that enables you to establish a base for the relationship. Let this person know what you do and of your interest in helping her or him do the job. Be honest and self-disclosing about what you see as the strengths and needs of the work unit, and chances are good you will be seen as a valuable player. Too many people make the mistake of playing politics with new bosses and try to see if they can manipulate them into seeing things their way. This makes the new person's job more difficult, and your actions are likely to lead to a sense of mistrust. While early on you may be able to influence a new boss who does not yet know what's really going on, chances are your manipulaton will hurt you in the long run. Your best tack is to give your new boss a realistic view of what's going on. If you find once you've done this that your perspectives are compatible, chances are your relationship will be a good one. If you find that you and your new boss have vastly different interpretations of reality, your best bet is to get out before things get worse. A bad match is a bad match, no matter how hard you try to change it. You might as well get out gracefully rather than prolong the agony that a bad relationship will inevitably cause.

When Your New Boss Is Your Old Friend   There's one other situation I'd like to talk about in relation to new bosses: what to do when that new boss is a former colleague. It happens all the time. Someone in your work unit moves up, and that someone isn't you.

The difficulty of this problem depends to a great extent on how competitive you are. If your colleague's success is a blow to your ego, your recovery will be slow and painful. If you feel that someone else's success is not a reflection of your lack of accomplishment, chances are much stronger that the relationship will remain a viable, sustained friendship.

As long as you can sort facts from feelings, you have an opportunity to use this event to your full advantage. Many a career has been built on the coattails of a friend. If you can separate fantasy from reality and get clear as to why the change occurred and what it means, you can emerge from this situation unscathed.

You have two choices here. The first is to accept your friend's success graciously, congratulate your new boss, and let him or her know you are committed to your work together. Make clear that you see this as an opportunity for both of you to grow and develop. It is likely that your friend, who is undoubtedly worried about the impact of the change on your relationship, will be relieved. Chances are good that your friend's success will enhance your success in the organization.

That's the first choice, which will work only if you are genuinely happy about and comfortable with your friend's success. If you see the change as a negative—either a reflection of the organization's lack of confidence in you or a realization that your career is not moving forward—then you need to treat the change as a signal for action. Nothing is more frustrating than watching colleagues move up as you remain stationary. At this point, you need to reassess your own progress and decide whether or not to make a move. If approached tactfully, your friend can help you with strategy. While you don't want to do this immediately, one way to take advantage of the situation is to share your feelings about the change with your friend in a way that opens up discussion of *your* career. Chances are your friend will be very willing to help because people often feel a little guilty about this kind of situation. This is a good time to explore with your new boss where you're headed. He or she is in an excellent position to sponsor you up the ladder, if that's what you want, or give you the support and leeway to make a move on your own, if that's what you want.

RESPONDING TO A CHANGE IN COMPANY OWNERSHIP

Symptoms

Once this phenomenon occurs, it is obvious; however, the symptoms of this condition begin prior to the actual transition.

If you see lots of strangers walking around the organization seeming particularly nosy and inquisitive, there's a good chance the company is up for grabs. An abundance of auditors (gray-suited people carrying thick ledgers) may also indicate your organization is about to change hands. If you work for a large organization, you may also find out about an imminent change of control through the newspapers.

Diagnosis

If you suspect your company is about to undergo a change in ownership, the sooner you begin to examine this potential change, the better. A change in ownership can mean many things—both good and bad—for the company itself and for the people who work there. If your organization is in trouble, an acquisition can sometimes save it, provided the purchaser is not a raider whose goal is to dismantle the company and sell off its parts. If the new ownership is the result of a merger, you'd better look carefully at who's buying and what they already do. Sometimes a merger brings disparate businesses together to form an entity stronger than either company was independently. If this is the case, it's entirely possible that your work will not be dramatically affected. In fact it may increase your resources and make your job more attractive. However, sometimes a merger brings similar businesses together to consolidate efforts and blend markets. If this is the case, you could be in for a shock. You may find out that you are no longer needed because the parent company already has enough people who "do what you do."

Another less obvious issue has to do with the goals, values, and standards of the new owners. Consider the small business for a moment. You may work for a small business whose owner is the founder of the company. Quite often the founder of the company will treat the company and its employees with kid gloves—nurturing the organization and its people so that the organization will grow and prosper. That person may decide—after a period of growth—to cash in the chips, reap the benefits of hard work, and sell the company to some other entrepreneur. It is likely that the new owner, who doesn't have the emotional investment that accompanies the growing of a business, will see the new acquisition more as a financial investment and run the company in a way that maximizes short-term profit rather than long-term stability. These two different approaches to managing the same business would create dramatically different work environments with dramatically different expectations, performance standards, and work conditions. If you were personally invested in the quality of life and attention to standards of the original company, you may find yourself unwilling to compromise and adapt to the new standards.

Consider the same scenario in a large company. For example, in recent years many publishing companies have been bought up by larger entertainment conglomerates. For years people in the publishing business prided themselves on the quality of the books their company produced. Many people in the industry now find that decisions around quality are very difficult to control as the parent company increasingly determines what will and will not be published. Many report that decisions around publication are increasingly made on the basis of factors other than quality.

While you may or may not care about some of these concerns, you should be aware of the fact that when company ownership changes, many things change with it.

Prognosis

As alluded to earlier, the outcome of new ownership will be determined by what drives the new owners. If the change of ownership strengthens the company's economic base but does not dramatically change its primary thrust, things will probably get only better. If the change of ownership changes the motives of those who control the purse strings, chances are good that your satisfaction with your work will be determined by the extent to which your personal goals are aligned with those of the "new" company.

Prescription

Pay attention to any rumblings of change. Even the slightest hint can alert you to a possible transfer of ownership. If you suspect a change is imminent, begin investigating possibilities discreetly but thoroughly. As with reorganizations, the best time to make a case for your future involvement with the company is before any formal plans have been solidified. A word of caution: Upon finding themselves in danger of losing their job as the result of a forthcoming change in company ownership, many people adopt a defensive posture and do all they can to secure their future with the company. This can be premature if you haven't yet gotten a handle on the nature of the changes that will accompany a change in ownership. It's entirely possible that after exploring the imminent change, you will decide it's time for you to make a move—out of the company. It's better to decide this and use the time when the company is in transition to look for other work rather than protecting a job you no longer want. Finding your place in a newly purchased company can be just as difficult as finding your place in a new organization. There's no reason to put yourself through that trauma twice unnecessarily. If getting out is ultimately what you're going to do, it's better to do it before the transition occurs rather than afterwards. You'll most likely have more energy for the search, and you'll most likely get more support in the way of job search assistance and references from long-term colleagues than from the new management.

For example, if you were the artistic director of a small advertising agency and your agency was bought up by a larger one, you might manage to stay on with the company. However, you would most likely not retain your position as artistic director; you would probably find yourself a member of a larger design staff. The question you should be asking yourself is not "How do I keep my job?" The question should be "Am I willing to make a shift from managing my own shop to becoming a member of another director's stable of designers?" Your answer to this question will determine whether you should work toward gaining a commitment from the new management or toward planning your departure from the organization.

If, after careful examination, you decide that the organization under new ownership looks good to you, it's time to strategize around finding your niche in the new company. Remember that you're not alone. If you've been a valued member of the organization, there are most likely numerous people willing to help you find a place that's a good match. Begin talking with everyone involved about the imminent change. The higher up you can go, the better. These are the people privy to the most information. Find out what the new ownership is like, what their priorities are, what their style is, and any idiosyncrasies they might have. Have conversations about the nature of the likely changes and explore ways you might be able to contribute to the implementation of those changes. Consider approaching management with a plan for your future role as soon as you think you have a realistic one. Don't "wait and see where they put you." Remember, if you don't have a plan for yourself, you'll probably become part of someone else's plan. The chances of your liking their plan as much as your own are slim. If you can think of a way of contributing to the goals of the new owner in a way that matches your own needs, you're on your way to surviving the transition and thriving under the new leadership.

WHEN YOU FIND YOURSELF THE CAPTAIN OF A SINKING SHIP

Symptoms

This can happen under two sets of conditions: You may find yourself in charge of a work unit that has been slated for destruction, or you may find yourself hired to save a ship that's in danger of sinking. In either case you will know this is happening when you find your resources dwindling and your access to key organizational players diminishing.

Diagnosis

The first thing to pay attention to is the severity of the threat. Is your unit being challenged to justify its existence, or is its demise all but inevitable? Regardless of the circumstances, you need to be careful here. The conventional wisdom that the captain should go down with the ship can leave your career in shambles. While there may be times to choose to stick with it for the long haul, there are other times when you need to protect yourself by moving within or out of the organization.

Prognosis

If a rescue is possible and desirable, this could be the perfect opportunity to establish yourself as an organizational superstar. Saving a work unit that's in trouble and turning a poorly functioning work group into a high-performing one can secure you a special place in the company and enable you to write your own ticket throughout the organization. Then again, presiding over the imminent demise of a work unit can establish you as one of the losers and prevent you from getting any decent assignments in the future. What's required here is a thorough assessment of the situation, an analysis of your options, and a careful strategy that ensures that you don't go down with the ship.

Prescription

If you've been in charge of the work unit in question for a while, plans for its elimination should come as no surprise to you. If they are a surprise, it's an indication that you should be paying closer attention than you have been. Likewise, if you've just taken a position to oversee a department's elimination and you didn't realize that was the case, it suggests that your interviewing skills leave much to be desired.

In any event, such things can come as a surprise. What's important is that you take action as soon as you realize what's happening. The first thing you need to do is to determine whether or not the vessel is salvageable. You do this by probing those responsible for overseeing your operation to see if there's any chance of patching things up and becoming sea-worthy again. If there is, you need to decide whether you're up to the challenge and proceed accordingly. If there's no chance of salvage, you need to take care of yourself and those who report to you to make sure to the extent possible that all parties, including you, are assigned to lifeboats or are at least given life preservers to enable them to stay afloat until they can find safety.

If you find in your investigation that the unit is saveable and the task seems manageable, you should embrace the opportunity. Pulling a work unit out of a difficult, threatening situation can be extremely valuable to your career both within this organization and beyond. People who can demonstrate their ability to turn problem situations around are coveted, and you will find your marketability enhanced dramatically because of this notch on your resume. You'll also find that if you manage to pull a dying work unit out of the fire those you've saved will be extremely grateful and loyal to you. Chances are that after the crisis, your tenure in that organization will be extremely productive and fruitful because of the kind of performance your actions will generate in those who report to you.

The oft-quoted Japanese maxim that "crisis equals danger and opportunity" holds much relevance here. Proving that you are someone who can take a potentially dangerous situation and turn it into an opportunity will enrich your career and give you a reputation worth more than the most impressive creden-tial. Choose to embrace this philosophy—carefully, when the odds are in your favor—and you'll find yourself a revered captain with many ships from which to choose.

WHEN THE FLATTENING HIERARCHY SQUASHES YOUR JOB

Symptoms

While similar to reorganization, this particular change is unique in many ways and warrants special attention. Flatten-

ing hierarchies are "in." There is no doubt that the trend in America is the shrinking of middle management and the elimination of layers between those at the top and those at the bottom. The best way to identify this is to look at what happens to the organizational chart during a restructuring. Most traditional organizational charts look like pyramids with the CEO at the top followed typically by at least seven or eight layers of reporting relationships. When the flattening hierarchy phenomenon clicks in, you're likely to see the elimination of at least two or three levels in the pyramid.

Diagnosis

At worst you could find yourself absent from the pyramid, in which case it's time to look for work, and the impact of the flattened hierarchy on how the organization operates is of little concern. If you survive the shift in the pyramid, you can be sure that the nature of your work—and your relationships to other people in the organization—will change dramatically. You can expect several things from this shift in organizational style. The first difference is confusion. This kind of change tends to blur roles and relationships. People become confused about what is now expected of them. Next is fear. People begin to worry about what this shift in the distribution of power will do to their own ability to get their jobs done. Finally, people experience anger and frustration over what they percieve to be a simultaneous decrease in their authority and increase in their overall responsibility.

Prognosis

As with any major change, you have a choice. You can resist the organizational shift and postpone the inevitable change in personal style that organizations with flattened hierarchies demand, or you can embrace the change, learn new ways of operating, and focus your energy instead on figuring out what the new configuration means about how you do your work. If you choose to work with the change rather than against it, chances are good that you will be able to survive and thrive in the streamlined organization.

Prescription

If you find yourself in this situation and you're anywhere near what your organization would consider middle management, the first thing you probably need to contend with is a sense of loss. Many middle managers report that this restructuring feels as if their "heads were in a vise." The reason for this is that flattening hierarchies create demands on middle managers that can be very difficult to handle. For one thing, your authority is lessened. With the flattened hierarchy comes the expectation

that you become a more participatory manager than you previously were. This means you have to delegate more and that
you have less power over the actions of those who report to
you. At the same time your accountability is expanded, those
who may have served as a buffer between you and upper-level
management have likely been eliminated. You have less control than you used to and also more responsibility, which
explains the feeling of being trapped.

The good news is that all of this is not as grim as it seems.
What's required is an understanding of the potential for an
organization with flattened hierarchies—and the potential for
those working in one. It's no fluke that the trend toward flattened hierarchies is taking corporate America by storm. If you
find yourself in the midst of this kind of organizational trans-
formation, it's important to understand how it works. One of
the reasons many people resist the change is that it forces them
to discard old habits in favor of new ones. In order for the
restructured organization to function well, several changes
need to occur. Procedures for just about everything need to be
streamlined, eliminating all unnecessary steps. People need to
talk with each other more candidly and openly than they ever
did before, up, down, and across the hierarchy. A climate of
mutual trust must be established and maintained. Finally, a
philosophy of internal collaboration must be supported
throughout the organization in lieu of any former norms
around internal competition.

While you cannot single-handedly create this sort of organizational change, you can contribute to its implementation—
and solidify your role in the "new" organization. Chances are
that if the company is serious about improving through flattening the hierarchy, the leaders already know what kinds of
changes need to take place. What you need to do is show that
you understand the shifting dynamics and are willing and able
to support them. Begin by examining your work unit's ways of
operating and start making recommendations for streamlining
everything possible. Start talking to people in other departments about ways you can make each others' jobs easier, and
keep management informed of your conversations and

your progress. Let other people know how much you want to work together with them to make the new configuration work, and show them in as many ways as you can that you are operating in good faith. Finally, realize that although you may lose some authority in the short run the power you gain from empowering others around you to do their best will more than make up for the loss of being able to tell people what you want them to do.

If you embrace the spirit of participation and involvement that flattening hierarchies offer, you will find that the company will most likely value your contribution and, if necessary, find a new job for you if your old one was eliminated. Most important to realize is that a streamlined, cooperatively based, high-performing company can be a very exciting place to work—and can provide invaluable experience for future career moves.

WHEN THE BOSS'S SON GETS THE JOB YOU'VE BEEN WAITING FOR

Symptoms

Finding yourself losing out on a promotion you thought was coming requires careful scrutiny. You don't want to assume that you didn't get it because someone else was more deserving. It may be that you didn't get it because someone else was more connected. Family connections, for example, can interfere with your ascension in an organization. Competition from "the boss's son" may just be the tip of the iceberg. While you might expect to have to take second place to the leader's offspring, you might be surprised to find other family members preempting your progress as well.

Diagnosis

Many organizations have norms around family involvement. Some companies shy away from familial involvement, and some embrace it. One simple way to figure out how "family friendly" an organization may be is to look for recurrent appearances of the same names on the organizational chart. If you see a lot of repetition, you've found an organziation that supports family involvement in it. This may or may not be a problem. It can be a problem if those at the top have a vested interest in seeing their relatives rise in the organization ranks to the point where the family factor overrides the performance factor when it comes to promotions.

Prognosis

Many companies that support the leader's family are good places for outsiders to work as well. What matters are the criteria and priorities on which promotions are based. It's entirely possible to work for a company with strong family ties that also has high standards for measuring performance. If the organization is equitable and ethical in its promotion practices, there's no reason to fear strong family connections. In these organizations those in power make it clear to those moving up that the bottom line for their promotion—whether they're insiders or outsiders—is performance. If you find yourself working in one of these organizations, focus your energy on outperforming the relatives—not outmaneuvering them—and you shouldn't have a problem.

If you're surprised by the upward mobility of seemingly low-performing colleagues, you've probably stumbled into an organization where family history means more than work history. Your best bet is to move to another organization that has more controllable criteria for success.

Prescription

Identifying potential family-based obstacles in an organization begins with your first contact with the company. In general, larger organizations are less likely to be family driven than smaller ones, although there are some large companies with strong family histories as well. Begin your scrutiny of this potential obstacle when you first consider taking a position, and you're less likely to be unpleasantly surprised down the line. Make observations and ask questions in your initial contact with an organization: Who holds the power positions in the organization? On what basis are promotions made? What are the performance standards? What is the ethnic-cultural makeup of the organization? Are there any familial patterns discernible from the company roster? While some of these questions are askable, some of them require keen observation skills. Regardless of how you get the answers to these questions, having this information will clue you in on the extent to which family connections are likely to interfere with your success in the organization.

So far I've been talking about prevention, that is, how to avoid getting your progress cut short by others' genealogical advantage. However, you still may find yourself—if you weren't careful or if the pattern is carefully masked—the victim of family privilege that is preventing you from getting you where you want to be . The main problem with this dilemma is that it is not an issue that can be confronted head-on because those responsible for perpetuating it often feel justified in their actions. They may even be unaware of it and acting on the basis of subtle, subconscious interpretations of situations that support family members' advancement over outsiders.

If you believe—or know—that you've been passed over for promotion in favor of someone with a family connection, you should take the situation very seriously and assess whether it is a signal that it's time for you to move on. You should approach the person responsible for making the decision against you and pursue (in a very tactful way) the implications of their actions. Whatever you do, don't accuse them of nepotism or favoritism unless you're ready to hand in your resignation at the end of the conversation.

During the conversation you should focus on your own situation, your concern about not getting the anticipated promotion, and the implications of that decision. You need to be careful not to make accusations or suggestions about any impropriety in their decision. However, if you focus their attention on the decision that was made, you open up the possibility of learning about the basis for their decision. If the person who did receive the position had some qualifications that you were unaware of, you may learn something that explains the situation that goes beyond family connection. If this happens, you can breathe more easily, knowing that your chances are not hopelessly affected by your lack of relation. If the decision was based on family connection, however, the conversation you're in, if you listen carefully, will often reveal that. People give themselves away by what they say and don't say about these matters. Comments like "I'm not sure you understand how we do things around here" or "We feel that we're the best judge of who gets promoted when" suggest that familial privilege is alive and well in this organization.

If you feel from the initial feedback you're getting from this conversation about why you got passed over that there are no family-based red flags popping up, you may want to pursue the question of future plans. Letting management know that you are concerned about your ability to move up after being passed over gives them an opportunity to state their intentions regarding your future. While you want to be careful not to put them on the spot, this is a good time to find out if you should hang in longer or should be fine-tuning your resume. While it's unlikely you'll get any sort of formal commitment at this point, if they value you and see you as potentially a key player in the future, they will most likely let you know. Noncommital comments like "We're sorry you're disappointed; better luck next time" should send you directly to "the perfect resume" software you might already own. Any savvy manager knows that employees who've been passed over for promotions they really wanted are inclined to leave. If they intend to move you up, they'll let you know—in some way—that it's probably worth your while to stay on and that they'll do what they can to make sure you aren't passed over again. While you can't expect a commitment, you can expect some support. Comments like "We understand your disappointment and will carefully monitor the situation so that the next time something appropriate comes along you get a fair shot at it" signify hope. While this might still leave you with a bad taste in your mouth for having lost an opportunity, it does suggest that, while family may get preferential consideration, there is room for growth for all players—including you.

THE LOYALTY FACTOR

Symptoms

Loyalty is a tricky thing. Many people consider it a virtue, yet at times it can get you in trouble and lead to an inappropriate relationship between you and your organization or between you and other people in your organization. Other people consider it a waste and disparage it as something to be avoided. Most people have fairly clear-cut standards about loyalty. You know you have a loyalty dilemma when your usual standards are challenged and you're faced with a situation that feels uncomfortable regardless of the decision you make.

Diagnosis

The reason loyalty issues are so difficult to handle is that they force you to deal with the unpredictable. Questions around loyalty come into play when the limits of a realtionship are stretched to the point where you don't know what to do. The key to determining a course of action is to assess the extent to which your loyalty compromises other values like honesty, integrity, and ethics.

Prognosis

The biggest dangers concerning the loyalty factor are whether to choose loyalty over all other factors or to forgo loyalty entirely in favor of other standards. What this does is make you extremely vulnerable to poor judgment calls that can leave you wishing you had chosen some other course of action. While appropriate acts of loyalty can lead to a reciprocal relationship between you and your organization that creates a healthy alliance, blind loyalty can compromise you in ways that can cause you harm. Similarly, the decision to dismiss loyalty as a useless phenomenon limits your potential to create mutually beneficial relationships. The key to handling the loyalty factor is to maintain a clear perspective and make judgments based on an understanding of the total picture and the implications of your actions rather than on the assumption that loyalty is the best policy or the worst policy.

Prescription

When it comes to the loyalty factor, people seem to cluster at two extremes. Many people take their own level of loyalty for granted, having been raised on the notion that displaying un-wavering commitment to your organization is the only way to be, a throwback to the "organization man" concept promoted in the 1950s. These people feel compelled to stand by their organization regardless of its actions. For others, this overrid-ing sense of devotion is on the wane, the victim of increasingly volatile organizations that seem unable to offer loyalty in re-turn. The problem is that either position represents an extreme and does not allow for the complexity that most questions around loyalty pose.

For those with a tendency toward a lack of organizational loyalty, the challenge is to realize the value inherent in a mutu-ally satisfying loyalty pact with an organization. This sort of unspoken arrangement to be reciprocal in your support of each other can be the basis for a long, fruitful relationship. When this sort of connection is completely absent, the result is a decided sense of insecurity on both parts. Neither party knows what they can expect from the other, and the likelihood of both parties getting their needs met is diminished. So even if your "free spirit" sensibilities guide you toward a lack of commitment to any one organization you owe it to yourself and to those you work for to give them a sense that you are interested in a "win-win" proposition in the relationship.

For those of you on the other side of the loyalty fence, the challenge is to realize the prudence of selective loyalty—that is, being careful not to put your faith in loyalty that is irrational or ill advised. The sort of loyalty I'm talking about here is the kind that can hurt you. It can manifest itself in many ways. Refusing to believe that your job is at stake when a company is reorganizing or changing hands, refusing to acknowledge that your company is making a poor judgment call, and turning your back when your company does something immoral, illegal, or unethical are examples of how misguided loyalty can cause you grief.

The biggest problem with the loyalty factor—on both sides of the fence—is that people tend to develop unconditional positions on where they stand. For example, it's not unusual to hear people faced with a decision they regret saying, "I guess I'm just too loyal." This statement is very revealing in that it suggests that your behavior in response to loyalty issues is unchangeable. On the other side of the fence is the person who eschews loyalty and proclaims, "I never trust anyone." Both of these people are operating on the assumption that their position on issues such as loyalty are "right" enough to carry them comfortably through any situation. The reality is that decisions concerning loyalty require careful judgments that are based on the circumstances and intricacies of a given situation. Limiting your behavior to a predetermined philosophy leaves you vulnerable to making a bad decision.

The best approach is to realize that loyalty can be an extremely powerful force when practiced in an appropriate way and that there are times when it's better to make judgments that challenge loyalty in light of more compelling factors. Keep your options open, your thinking clear, and your judgment flexible, and chances are you will appreciate both the benefits and limitations of the loyalty factor.

WHEN THE ORGANIZATIONAL CULTURE MAKES YOU FEEL LIKE A FOREIGNER

Symptoms

By now most people know that all organizations have cultures. What many still deny is that culture is a key variable influencing success in an organization. Most people are more comfortable focusing on their ability to do the job and the organization's need for their services as the key determinants of their success. Because culture is such a difficult thing for any one individual to influence, the thought that the organization's culture might be your undoing is a frightening thing.

Knowing that you're having culturally based problems in an organization is a simple thing. A sense of lingering uneasiness over not fitting in is a sure sign that you're having a difficult time integrating into the organization's culture. When you're part of a bad match, you may very well feel a sense of alienation similar to finding yourself in a country where people speak a language different from your own.

Diagnosis

When it comes to a cultural mismatch, there are many levels at which the problem might exist. If the differences between you

and the organizational culture are based in core values, like worldview, attitudes about work, or philosophical, moral, and ethical perspectives, then the challenge is a formidable one. If the differences have more to do with surface issues concerning organizational rituals, patterns, and traditions, your task may merely involve reeducating yourself around patterns of behavior.

Prognosis

If you find yourself in an organization that seems compatible with you in its point of view but you feel awkward with the outward manifestations of that point of view, chances are that with a little homework you can bridge the gap between yourself and the organization's dominant culture. If you find yourself repelled by or in conflict with the organization's espoused values and positions around key issues, however, it is unlikely that you will be able to reconcile those differences. Organizational culture is a powerful force influencing everthing and everyone in an organization. It is unlikely that any one person can change an organization to more closely match their personal perspectives.

Prescription

The first thing to be careful about is not to downplay the importance of a cultural match on your career. Most people focus on the match between their skills and abilities to do the job rather than on their match with the organization. The problem with this is that finding yourself at odds with the organization's culture will create an internal conflict that will gradually eat away at your comfort and sense of fitting in the organization. This discomfort will eventually have an impact on your ability to do your job. If you don't confront the issue honestly and gain an accurate assessment of your compatibility with the organization, you'll find yourself compensating for differences in ways you are not even aware of. The impact of

the mismatch will be that your work is harder, your relationships strained, and your chances of performing optimally
diminished. Like many other conditions, the best approach
here is prevention. Identifying a mismatch before you join an
organization will save you the grief of leaving—or forcing yourself to live in a hostile environment.

Unfortunately, most people don't pay attention to their compatibility with an organization's culture until they're a part of
it. Getting into a job creates so much anxiety that most people
focus too intently on their willingness and ability to do the job,
their compensation package, and the viability of the organization they're approaching to pay much attention to culture. If
you can, it makes sense to focus on your way in—even briefly—on the culture question. Can you support the organization's vision, mission, goals, and objectives? Do you respect
the product or service the organization produces? Are the
kinds of people who work there the kinds of people you are
drawn to or at least find interesting? Are the organization's
explicit and implicit expectations about patterns of behavior
acceptable to you? Answers to these questions will alert you as
to whether this organization's culture is compatible with who
you are. It's important not to mistake these key cultural variables for incidental ones like the way people dress, norms
around social interaction, or rituals for celebrating significant
events. While these factors can give you insight into the ways
of the organization, for most people they do not make or break
cultural considerations.

If you have the presence of mind to pay attention to cultural
considerations prior to accepting a job, you might avoid making a poor decision based on cultural incompatibility. Chances
are, however, that you'll discover the incompatibility once
you're already in the organization and resistant to making a
move. The important thing to do here is to make a distinction
between cultural differences that are changeable and those that
are not. For example, one powerful factor in compatibility is
personal alignment with the product or service your organization delivers. Successful salespeople will tell you that a key to
their success is that they believe in the quality of the product or

service they deliver. Without that belief, you have to muster a tremendous amount of energy to do the work. Eventually the lack of commitment to and belief in the product or service will inhibit your performance and affect your success negatively.

If you find yourself feeling like a foreigner in your organization, the first and most important thing is to figure out the source of that feeling. Don't assume that you're a misfit or a round peg in a square hole until you've determined the origins of your discomfort. If the language of the country you're in is the problem, you can most likely learn the language with the help of an interpreter until you feel comfortable. If it's the underlying assumptions about what's important in life, the chances of your changing your perspective, adapting to, and feeling comfortable in your new environment are minimal.

In any event, the key to bridging the culture gap is determining the basis for the gap and identifying whether you merely need some reeducating or whether you need an entirely new environment to work in.

COPING WITH PLATEAUING

Symptoms

A distinct feeling that you have nowhere to go in your organization and an affirmation of that feeling when you look at the organizational chart and see no next step up on it for you are sure signs that your career has reached a plateau.

Diagnosis

No career is immune to plateaus. In fact, it would be highly unlikely that you would go through your entire career without periodically encountering a plateau. The problem with the term "plateau" is that it usually has a negative connotation. People concerned with losing weight talk about a plateau as the point at which they stop losing weight and have to do something to rekindle their calorie burning. Many people think of a plateau as a level point at which they have ceased to progress. In reality a plateau in your career can be a positive thing if you are able to allow yourself the freedom to operate at a sustained level.

Prognosis

Whether a plateau in your career represents a threat or an opportunity depends on the nature of the plateau and the context in which it surfaces. If you find your ascent in an organization suddenly cut off by unforeseen factors, a plateau could require dramatic action on your part. However, if you've been rapidly moving up in your organization and you find your progress slowed, this may be an opportunity to fine-tune your skills and develop some mastery in an area that will help your career get through difficult times down the road. Many people who are concerned with moving up as fast as possible fail to develop a depth of skill or knowledge along the way that would make their talents more transferrable in the future. A career plateau may be the perfect time to develop your competence in a specialty area. Achieving performance excellence in some aspect of your field can provide the linchpin for future transitions.

Prescription

The first thing you need to do is to discern the cause of the plateau. Is it the result of a rapid rise to the top that is being slowed by those above you to allow them time to reap the benefits of your developing talent, the result of some artificial barrier that exists in your organization, or a symbol of the limits of future opportunity for you?

If the plateau occurs in the context of a rapid rise that shows every indication of continuing, you may be wise to accept it as a natural part of your progression and use it as a time to reflect, regroup, and rejuvenate. Time well spent on a plateau can be used to develop your competence and reputation in your specialty. Remember, nothing can enhance your career more than being able to do what you do better than anyone else in the business. A plateau period can be just the time to develop your expertise beyond that of those with whom you are competing in the marketplace.

If the plateau is the result of some artificial barrier that exists in your organization, you may have to take action. The glass ceiling that reportedly exists for women in many organizations is a perfect example of such a barrier. The glass ceiling refers to the situation in some organizations in which women can see the next steps in the hierarchy but are not able to reach them because of organizational bias against women. If you find yourself plateaued by an artificial barrier like the glass ceiling, it may be that your plateauing is a signal that it's time for you to move on to another organization where that barrier doesn't exist or is more permeable.

If your plateauing is a symbol of the limits of future opportunity, your task is the most challenging. The first thing you need to do is assess your level of satisfaction with your current position. If you are satisfied with the nature and level of your work and your level of compensation, then it may be that the plateau you've reached reflects a level of stability in your career. There's nothing wrong with deciding that you like what you do and would enjoy continuing doing it for the rest of your career—or at least for an extended period of time. Too many people, obsessed with upward mobility, fail to recognize or admit that where they are feels good. Our society contains far too many messages that suggest that if you're not moving up you're going nowhere. However, if where you are is where you want to be, why not stay there a while?

If you find yourself on a plateau and you've not yet achieved a reasonable degree of satisfaction and comfort with what you do and are not on the level you want to be, with its accompanying compensation package, then you've got your work cut out for you. In this scenario the problem is not how to rise above your current level; it's confronting the fact that you may be in a field or profession that does not offer you the rewards you want. This lack of potential may be the result of changing demographics, that is, too many people wanting the same position; shifting economics, such as fewer companies providing the kinds of services you offer in your geographic range; or technological advances, such as lessened demand for people who perform the sort of work you do.

If you find, once you examine the causes of your plateauing, that you are left with nowhere to go in your field, you are faced with the reality that the only way to get beyond the plateau is to shift the nature of what you do dramatically or change the arena in which you do it and change careers. This is a decision that should not be made lightly. Before you decide, you had better examine your situation carefully and make sure your sense of dissatisfaction with being plateaued is not a temporary condition that will remedy itself if you hang in long enough. If you decide to change careers, you should be sure that where you're headed is better than where you've been in terms of providing you with what is important to you.

If there are aspects of your current work that you really enjoy and are really good at, you want to be careful in your transition not to "throw the baby out with the bathwater." If you decide to make a career change to get off your plateau, carefully consider what aspects of your current work you want to retain in your new work and make a move that allows you to keep those priorities intact.

Many people think that a career change means starting from scratch. However, the most successful career changers are those who bring their best stuff with them. Make a careful move, one that takes advantage of your greatest strengths and offers greater opportunity, and you may soon experience the pleasure of viewing your old plateau from a new peak.

FOUR

Political Problems You Need to Control

Political problems related to your career management can un-
ravel an otherwise healthy career if you are not aware of their
potential or don't recognize them when they surface. Career-
related politics have to do with problems that cannot be resolved through other, less complex means. Your skills and
talents will not save you from political threats, nor will your
position in the organization. Strong communication skills
won't even protect you from these problems—although they
will help in the implementation of your plan to combat the
political threat.

THE PICTURE OF HEALTH: POLITICAL WELLNESS

Your career is politically healthy when you've developed a
means for anticipating, responding to, and neutralizing situations that threaten your career. Political health involves an
appreciation of the potential impact of political maneuvers on
your career and the development of a set of skills to handle
them. Part of this is attitude. The "I hate politics" attitude will
get you nowhere and likely lead you into trouble because of the
"wearing blinders" approach it takes to political situations.
People who don't like the messiness of political problems go to
great lengths to avoid them, often pretending they don't exist.
Anyone at all familiar with organizational dynamics will tell
you that politics are everywhere. Some observers suggest that
anytime you have more than two people together you have a
political situation; others say that more than one person con-
stitutes a political situation. To grasp the complexity of this
situation, we need to examine what we're really talking about
when we use the word "politics." In fact, by simply looking at
definitions we can get at some of the controversy surrounding
the concept. Those who have a disdain for politics probably
embrace the meanings that shed a negative light as in one
dictionary's "crafty, unscrupulous, and cunning." Such a view
of politics is likely to lead to a discrediting of the phenomenon
as something to be avoided. Those who do run a great risk, one
that will be detrimental to their political wellness. The political-

ly healthy professional knows that regardless of personal preferences the notion that organizational politics can have an impact on your career is an important reality, not a choice. Your decision is whether to accept the reality and work with it or to deny the reality, resist it, and make yourself vulnerable to its workings. Consider the less sinister definitions of politics as an appropriate view for political wellness in your career: "artful, ingenious, wise, prudent, and judicious."

The politically healthy professional sees the task of managing the politics of careers as a challenge—one that requires astute attention to the subtleties and inner workings of organizations and their inhabitants. The politically healthy professional knows the nature of both organizational and marketplace politics, has developed a successful way of functioning in the context of those politics, and is prepared to deal with unanticipated problems that emerge as a result of them.

WHAT TO DO IF YOU GET BLACKBALLED

Symptoms

Finding yourself on the outs within an organization or having an unusually difficult time getting into an organization may be signs that you are being blackballed. The term refers to a state of affairs in which you feel—and are—ostracized, that is, intentionally excluded from an organization or group. Whether it occurs while you're in an organization or in the marketplace trying to gain access to an organization, you need to confront this problem aggressively or it will cause irreparable harm to your career.

Diagnosis

Blackballing can be difficult to diagnose because it is by design a secretive phenomenon. It is unlikely that anyone supporting your being blackballed is going to advertise their position in what is often an emotionally charged and potentially litigious situation. People who willingly admit to participating in black-balling you are opening themselves up to potential attack and lawsuits. This reality supports the notion that you had better sharpen your political skills, which are the main skills that can help you when you find yourself the victim of a blackballing campaign.

Prognosis

The bad news is that if you refuse to "play politics," you may not even realize you're being blackballed while it's happening. The good news is that if you suspect there's a problem and you focus your efforts on finding out what it is and who is the source, chances are you can uncover the problem and the culprit. Blackballing is the kind of secret that many people can't seem to help talking about, despite their better judgment that they should keep quiet. If you put your feelers out and really pay attention to what's going on around you, you'll most likely find out what's happening and who's behind it.

Prescription

You should consider the possibility that you're being blackball-ed if you find yourself losing opportunities and can't find any other legitimate reason for your being rejected. In the case of blackballing, early awareness of the problem can be critical since it can prevent the institutionalizing of the situation or the widespread adoption of a negative attitude against you. If the position being taken against you occurs in the context of one organization, the danger is that it can strengthen with time and be impossible to undo. If it occurs in the career marketplace, the danger is that it will spread and you will find yourself unemployable in your chosen field.

Pinpointing the source of your problem is the first step. Identify who in your sphere of influence might have cause to lash out against you, and you've taken the first step toward eradicating the problem. If the problem is within an organization, focus on possible culprits at all levels. Don't assume the source of your trouble is above you. Peers and those below you in the hierarchy are very capable of poisoning your reputation in a way that can lead to your widespread unpopularity. If the problem is in the marketplace, don't assume that it's limited to just one organization. Negative campaigns can spread like wildfire. If you're being boxed out by one organization, there's a good chance other organizations are being influenced against you as well.

Once you've isolated the problem, it's time for action. While many people may be involved, probably one person is the primary source of your trouble. Make sure you've got the right person, and focus your efforts on resolving the problem with her or him. If you can successfully turn around the key person, everyone else will most likely fall into line. Your best approach is to start out informally. Talking with and trying to disarm this person can save you the time and energy of more complicated strategies. If the culprit is in an organization that you're working in and want to continue working in, your task is to get this person to stop getting in the way of your advancement. If you're in the job market and the person causing you grief is creating problems for you by providing negative information about you to prospective employers, your task is to get this person to change what he or she is saying about you. If you've successfully isolated the problem and can stop the person responsible from getting in your way, you've managed to turn a potential disaster into a minor inconvenience. Chances are, however, that if you've been getting blackballed by this person, friendly conversation alone will not solve your problem. You may need to get progressively tougher in your approach. If you feel your one-to-one conversations are not getting you the results you want, your next step should be to try to get those who have an influence on this person to influence him or her toward leaving your future alone. A careful and thorough lobbying effort may be just enough to get this person off your back.

Those are your informal options. If they don't work, it may be time to resort to more serious alternatives. You never want to go over someone's head unless you're ready to leave an organization or are resigned to never getting into that particular organization. However, if someone is causing your career undue harm by blackballing you, a formal complaint may be your only reasonable alternative. This involves approaching someone's superior with clear, well-documented information about an employee's efforts to limit your access to positions in the organization. This can work if you've had a good track record and have the ear of those at the top. It is more difficult to do this with an organization you are not yet a part of. In most cases, though, the source of your problem will be based in an organization you're already in or have recently left. Take care of this problem and there's a good chance you'll break the chain where it counts most—in the first link.

If your efforts to eliminate the problem by working with those above the culprit are unsuccessful and you're determined to put an end to what is described by some as covert harassment, your only remaining option is to use the most formal weapon you can in this situation—the law. If all else fails, get yourself a lawyer and have them send a letter to your identified blackballer and their superiors voicing your concern about their treatment of you. Oftentimes this alone will remedy the situation. If it doesn't, carefully pursue alternatives for further steps with your lawyer and take them. This could mean filing a suit based on defamation of character, discrimination, or a range of related complaints. A good lawyer can review your options with you and help you pursue the best path. While I hesitate as much as possible before turning to litigation—it's difficult and sometimes costly for all parties— when all else fails, it may be the only way to get yourself out from under the blackball.

KNOWING WHEN TO SAY NO

Symptoms

Finding yourself feeling decidedly ambivalent and uncomfortable over an important decision is a signal that you may be faced with the possibility of saying no to a proposition that has some merit to it.

Diagnosis

The reason this is a political problem is that your answer to a given proposition is not always obvious. If your preference is clear, it's because you're able to sort out the pluses and minuses of a situation and arrive at what you know to be the best response. When your sorting of pros and cons leaves you with no definitive response, you need to summon your intuitive faculties—that sense of judgment that guides you through difficult situations—to help you make a decision you can live with.

Prognosis

The difficulty with this sort of situation is that you often won't know, at the time of your decision, whether you'll be satisfied with the choice. If your decision was cut-and-dried, you probably won't think twice about it. The decisions I'm talking about here fall into the gray area—neither a yes nor a no is entirely satisfying and you will know for sure whether you made the best decision only once time passes and you have the benefit of hindsight.

Prescription

Before giving you specific advice on how to know when to say no, I'd like to tell you about a recent experience I had that exemplifies this kind of dilemma.

Taking the Risk of Saying No to Risk Taking A few weeks ago I got a call from a major video production and marketing company asking me if I was interested in participating in a video as an expert on risk taking. The woman I spoke with told me how much she enjoyed my article on risk taking in the *Wall Street Journal's Business Employment Weekly*. I enthusiastically said yes to her offer and was told that this call was an initial query and that they would be back in touch. Four weeks later I received a message on my voice mail from the production studio to see if I was available for a scheduled shoot. I was surprised by the call since I had not heard from my initial contact about details such as time commitment, financial reimbursement, and other conditions of the relationship. At the time I was negotiating with another company regarding these matters, so I had a fair understanding of how such things might be handled. When I called back my initial contact with my concerns, she said, "I thought I had made it clear in our initial conversation that your appearance would be on a voluntary basis." I remembered the conversation and knew that no such thing had been made clear. At that point I had no idea if her approach had been inadvertent or intentional. She quickly told me she was in the middle of a meeting and asked if she could call me back the next day. I spent that evening thinking about whether or not I wanted to participate "for free" and give my stuff away to a company that was going to sell the tape for $70 a copy. I was also hesitant since I was at the time negotiating with another smaller company to do similar work for a substantial fee. The woman called me back the next day, and I told her I thought she had contacted me for a business proposition and was surprised to find out that it was a volunteer proposition. She began to tell me about the visibility I would get, the million people the tape would be exposed to, and the possibility that many people would buy it. She also told me she would put any title I wanted under my name and my books in the bibliography at the end of the tape. At that point I felt myself getting increasingly uneasy about the voluntary nature of my participation and heard myself say to her, almost involuntarily, "I think I'll pass." She promptly said goodbye and hung up the phone.

As soon as I got off the phone, I felt I had made a terrible mistake. My other negotiations were still in the early stages and were not by any means definite commitments. Besides, this was one of the biggest companies. How could I say no to them? It took me several days to realize that I was dealing with the aftermath of a "knowing when to say no" decision. The more I thought about it, the more convinced I was that I had made a good decision. I felt that I had every right to be paid for my expertise and, as days passed, I grew confident that I would receive other offers in the future that would provide similar opportunity—with more appropriate remuneration. As time passed, I grew less and less regretful and increasingly satisfied that I had made a good decision in saying no. A week after declining to participate for free, I received a call from this same woman, asking me what I would charge to appear in the video. After brief negotiation we settled on a fee that was acceptable to both of us.

This story illustrates several factors that come into play when your best response to a seemingly attractive proposition is to turn it down. When faced with a difficult decision about an opportunity, the best thing to do is summon all your available resources:

- Generate a list—mental or actual—of all the reasons for saying yes.

- Generate a list of all the reasons for saying no.

- Compare the two lists and make the obvious choice if there is one.

- Review both lists for any hidden factors that may hold unusual weight.

- See if there is any one overriding factor that you feel more strongly about than all the others.

- Talk to people you trust about what you're thinking about doing.

- If logic fails, use your intuition and make a decision on the basis of what "feels" best at the moment you need to make the decision.

While the last step in this process may seem to contradict the earlier ones, it is crucial to your ability to say no. Saying no goes against conventional wisdom about taking advantage of opportunity. The old adage "A bird in the hand is worth two in the bush" can wreak havoc on the psyche of a person trying to say no to the wrong job and hoping the right one will come along. In reality, a bad new job can be worse than no job at all because it takes you that much further away from getting the right one.

If I had initially said yes to the video that I really wanted to say no to, I would have compromised my standards of business practice, resented being taken advantage of, and, worst of all, succumbed to the upwardly mobile pressure that says, "Opportunity knocks only once." In reality, if you're doing a good job of managing your career, opportunity knocks a lot more than once. Those who say yes to every opportunity become yes men and women, subject to the whim of those who would control their careers. Those who choose carefully maintain a level of integrity and control over their own fates that makes any particular opportunity pale in comparison.

DEALING WITH ATTITUDES ABOUT YOUR AGE

Symptoms

Age-related problems can plague you at any period in your life. People may think you're too young to deserve or be capable of handling a position or too old to be worth investing in. Like sexual politics, age-related politics can derail an otherwise healthy career. Age can have an impact on your advancement within an organization if you're seen as too young to handle responsibility or too old to keep on. It can hurt your career mobility if you are trying to find a fit that defies the age norms for the particular position or organization.

Diagnosis

The most common age-related problems occur on the two ends of the spectrum; either you're perceived as too young and

immature to handle a job or too old and tired to carry your own weight. The key here is perception. While chronological age can influence someone for or against you on paper, the real test is the person-to-person impression you make about your age as an asset or liability in performing your work. This is why I urge people never to place age-revealing information on a resume. Fifty-five on paper can seem very old, depending on the age of the reader, yet this person can look quite young and vibrant in person. If you're serious about getting past any age-related bias you might encounter, you'll do all you can to save any impressions an interviewer might have for the face-to-face meeting.

Prognosis

Age-related problems can be tricky. There is no doubt that there are people who, in spite of laws to protect you, will discriminate against you because of your age. Unless you catch them in the act, there's nothing you can do about this. You *can* influence those people who are marginal, however. These people, in spite of being well-meaning, may have stereotypical ideas in their minds about what it means to be a certain age. What separates these people from the true ageists is their potential for having their prejudices dispelled by your presentation of yourself. You can avoid age-related discrimination by developing very specific strategies for challenging that bias head-on when confronting potential age-related issues.

Prescription

American culture is full of clichés intended to limit people by segmenting them on the basis of age. "You can't teach an old dog new tricks," being "over the hill" or "wet behind the ears," or the popular sixties saying "never trust anyone over 30" are statements that reflect ageist attitudes from both ends of the spectrum. While many people may try to resist age-based stereotyping, the reality is that such clichés reflect built in cultural bias. By far the most damaging discrimination occurs against the older segments of the population. America is without a doubt a youth-oriented culture. Movies, books, television commercials, and magazine advertisements are mostly geared toward young Americans. Recent entries like the magazine *Lear's*, which is geared toward women over 40, suggest that there is some societal shift emerging, although the need for such a periodical itself points to the culture's obsession with youth. One hopeful development is that the demographics are slowly but surely changing. As the baby boom generation ages, this country will for the first time have its largest segment (in excess of 70 million people) entering their "golden years." This probably means that those in decision-making positions will be less likely to discriminate against older workers because they will need them to fill positions at all levels.

The developing population shift is probably of little consolation if you're one of those people who precedes the baby boomers or are at the head of the pack. If you're faced with age discrimination now and can't wait for the cultural transition, there are several things you can do. The most important thing is to realize that if you're not careful, other people's attitudes about your age can be most debilitating if you internalize those attitudes and start to believe them yourself. In my career-change workshops, I've had people as young as 35 tell me that they couldn't change careers because they were too old!

The healthiest attitude came from a 60-year-old woman who was thinking about going to law school. When she went home and told her family and friends, she received the kind of ageist response I've been talking about: "Do you realize that you'll be 64 when you get out?" Her response to them was, "I'll be 64 in four years whether or not I go to law school. The real question is, Do I want to be a lawyer and do I want to go through what it takes over the next four years in order to get there?" While she hasn't yet decided whether to do it, her early exploratory interviews with law schools have met with supportive responses.

Unless you're dealing with a flaming ageist, the response you get about your age will be determined greatly by your attitude about it and how you project that attitude. If the person you're approaching is at all open and you present yourself as motivated, energetic, and physically and mentally healthy, chances are good that your age won't work against you. If you come across as lethargic, apathetic, and worn out, chances are good that you'll be seen as someone who is too old for the challenge.

If you're at the other end of the spectrum—seen as too young for the level of responsibility you seek—your task is to show the other person that you have the maturity, the talent, and the experience to handle the job. Most important is to make sure that you don't overcompensate for your youth by projecting an overly arrogant impression—a sure turnoff.

If you believe you're suffering from negative attitudes about your age, your last resort—one to be used sparingly—is to consider an age discrimination suit. The problem with these suits is that they're very difficult to prove in court. They've also been misused by people who feel they have no other recourse for handling other situations in which they've been locked out. These suits are often viewed with suspicion by the courts and by employers—both present and future. Don't pursue this route unless you're prepared for a great deal of scrutiny and are willing to take the heat. Remember, in the long run your situation is a passing problem for an organization—but will remain a long-standing notch in your history.

WHEN YOUR BOSS PERCEIVES YOU AS A THREAT

Symptoms

If things have been going smoothly and you've been enjoying increasing success in your work, and then you find that there is suddenly mounting resentment or hostility from a superior, it may be that your boss is perceiving you as a threat. A sudden downturn in your boss's enthusiasm over your work when there has not been a downturn in your performance is a signal that you had better pay attention.

Diagnosis

You don't want to expend unnecessary energy on this sort of problem if you don't have to. This is a difficult condition to diagnose because there are many other potential problems whose symptoms can resemble the symptoms of this threat. One way to become clear on whether you're being too successful for your own good is to consider carefully other possibilities that could explain your boss's shift in attitude. For your boss, increased performance pressure, organizational changes, or personal problems can masquerade as discomfort with your positive performance.

Prognosis

If you are perceived as a genuine threat by a superior, you could find yourself in a no-win situation. Unless you can turn the situation around, you may be forced to look elsewhere for work. One possibility not to be eliminated is that if you're developing a good track record in the organization but your boss can't seem to handle your success, there may be some other place for you in the organization where you would be more appreciated. If there isn't and you're sure you've diagnosed the situation accurately, then your best bet is to move on and find someone more interested in moving you up, not holding you down.

Prescription

Because of the potential for misdiagnosis present in this situation, it is imperative that you examine the evidence before choosing a strategy and that you choose a strategy likely to alleviate the problem in the least disruptive way. Ideally what you want to change is not your job but the perception of threat on the part of your boss. Therefore, if you think you've got an accurate handle on the problem, first consider whether changing your behavior in minor ways might alleviate or eliminate the threat. Most often it is unwise to outshine your boss unless you're ready for and interested in a power struggle. In most cases making your boss look good will only contribute to your success. If you've been making yourself look good at your boss's expense, you may be choosing short-term glory in favor of long-term progress—an unfortunate choice.

If you believe you've inadvertently created a problem by outperforming your boss, it may be that all you need to do is figure out a way to share the glory and give your boss at least partial credit for your success. There is an unwritten rule in most organizations that employees' successes are not limited strictly to their own actions but rather are credits to those they report to as well. To violate this rule is to set yourself up for hostility from above. Finding a way to patch up the wrongdoing, such as publicly acknowledging your boss's contribution to your efforts or intentionally involving your boss in your activities, can cut short a potentially long-term and ultimately damaging complication for your career.

If you're after your boss's job—a scenario that should not be taken lightly—be prepared for a fight. Before entering into a power struggle to bypass a superior, make sure you're in an organization that is open to the possibility, make sure those above your boss are aware of your every move, and, most important, make sure you've got the goods.

WHY YOU SHOULD NEVER BURN YOUR BRIDGES

Symptoms

Feeling an intense desire to give someone who's given you a hard time a "taste of their own medicine" is a sure sign that you are about to burn a potentially valuable bridge. This is a problem because in a world that values information exchange and runs on informal networking, any bridge you burn could turn out, in the long run, to be the wrong one.

Diagnosis

Bridge burning is most likely to occur when you're leaving an organization. It can manifest itself in many ways. You may be tempted to launch a verbal attack, write a hostile letter of resignation, or engage in a smear campaign. Regardless of its form, it can have a potentially devastating impact on your career. When you burn your bridges, you set yourself up for potential retaliation by the person who got burned. The worst part is that you never know when or how they might strike back.

Prognosis

Reconstructing a damaged bridge can be difficult but well worth the effort in the long run. If you proceed carefully and delicately, chances are you can undo the damage. Like other situations that create damaging relationships, most often the people on both sides of the bridge are glad to see the conflict come to resolution.

Prescription

The best medicine here is prevention. Keep in mind what a small world it really is, and appreciate the possibility that creating an enemy on your way out of an organization may create all sorts of problems down the road when you find yourself crossing paths with that person again. The best thing you can do when dealing with someone with whom you clash is to minimize your contact with them until you're out of the organization. "If you can't say anything nice, don't say anything at all," may seem too sickeningly sweet under normal conditions, but considered in the context of your exit from an organization it makes a great deal of sense.

The Potential Peril of the Poison Pen Letter   One of the biggest mistakes perpetrated by bridge burners is the venomous letter of resignation. I understand that the written word is a powerful tool, and that many people find it therapeutic to bare their souls as their last official act upon leaving an organization. What I don't understand is how people rationalize such an act, given its potential for career damage. Think about being the recipient of such a letter and how you might feel hurt or attacked by the letter and its intent. Chances are that after a few days the impact would fade, and you would be left with a distinct relief that the person who wrote the letter is out of your life. In time, any pain you felt would most likely be replaced by a distasteful memory of the letter writer. However, I would predict that anytime you were asked about this person, your negative feelings would be conjured up and even your most neutral voice would suggest hostility. This is where the residual effects of the poison pen letter bear down on the future of the person who wrote it. Consider the fact that the recipient of your letter would in all probability be asked to provide a reference for you. It might be a written reference or more likely a telephone reference. The naive poison pen scribe thinks that the law will protect them from any slander brought on by the scorned recipient of the poison letter. While it is unlikely that you would ever have any concrete evidence that the person you'd attacked had retaliated, there are many ways for them to give a negative response to an inquiry without stating anything that would prove damaging in court. Consider the following scenario:

POTENTIAL EMPLOYER: I'm calling to do a reference check on Joe Smith. What can you tell me about his performance?

PREVIOUS EMPLOYER: I'd say Joe was *pretty* good at his job.

POTENTIAL EMPLOYER: Would you say without question that you would hire him again today?

PREVIOUS EMPLOYER: I'm not entirely sure I could give you an unconditional yes.

Case closed.

The previous employer has said nothing negative that would hold up in court, yet his noncommital responses have considerably diminished Joe's chances. Now, many of you may think that employers have become increasingly litigation conscious and have instructed employees to give no references beyond a verification of employment. While this policy could protect you from formal responses to your bridge-burning behavior, it would not, as illustrated in the previous scenario, protect you from informal responses that are damaging. In fact there is growing sentiment in corporate hallways that many executives, having been burned by the policy concerning silence regarding references, are becoming more candid. In an article on changing patterns regarding references in the *New York Times* (December 2, 1990), Claudia Deutsch reported that many executives now feel the silence surrounding references has gone too far and are urging employees in all corporations to talk more freely, informally, and through networks about candidates who are problematic.

You can be sure that if this trend toward openness continues your poison pen letter will haunt you far longer than it hurts the person to whom you wrote it. My advice on this is simple, yet seems to be therapeutic. If you must, write the poison pen letter. Make it as venomous as possible, place it in an envelope addressed to its target, and then burn it!

What to Do If You've Already Sent the Letter   Hindsight is wonderful but does you little good if you've already poisoned your prospects in writing. What you need to do now, if you want to undo the unwise deed, is to swallow your pride. Invite to lunch the people to whom you wrote the letter. If they say yes, meet with them, apologize for the letter, talk about what was going on for you that led you to do such an inappropriate thing, and ask that they put the experience behind them and, in essence, bury the hatchet. Whatever you do, be sure not to suggest in any way that they were partially to blame for your actions. This may be very difficult to do but is crucial to your getting past this difficult obstacle. If they seem to accept your apology with genuineness and grace, thank them for their openness, and be sure to write them a thank you letter after the meeting to reinforce your new relationship. Now this may all sound like a bit much for you—like bad-tasting medicine—but I've seen it work countless times.

If the target of your attack is still fuming from the assault and refuses to meet with you, your options are more limited. What I suggest you do in this case is to use those same writing skills that got you into trouble and write a letter of apology and conciliation. In your letter say all the same things I suggested be said in the lunch meeting in as clear and careful a way as possible. Again, be certain not to place blame on the other party for your actions. While this approach may not be as effective as a personal meeting, because you have no idea how the person is reacting, it can also help bury the hatchet and leave the person with a better feeling about you. If over time you suspect that the person is still holding a grudge, you may want to give the lunch meeting another shot. Important to remember in all of this is that you need to do all you can to retrace your steps and undo the damage. Remember, burned bridges make for bad business relations.

WHEN A PROMOTION MEANS INCREASED DISSATISFACTION

Symptoms

A prospective promotion is cause for celebration. If you find yourself hesitating and excessively nervous about the prospect of the change, it may be that your ascension up the ladder is really a descent into dissatisfaction.

Diagnosis

The best way to understand this puzzling situation is through illustration. The story that follows is but one example of a phenomenon that happens every day in every industry. If you're not careful, you could become its next victim.

Eric, the Impatient Engineer: A Case Study   Eric is a design engineer in the aerospace industry. His specialty is designing and modifying fuel-delivery systems for midsized airplanes. Eric thrives on his work. He loves sitting in a cramped corner of his lab solving technical problems and designing exquisitely precise instruments. His company loves him too. They are so fond of him and so concerned about keeping him that they decide to promote him to the position of "manager of engineering."

At first Eric was thrilled with the recognition and professional validation that the promotion reflected. He immediately accepted the promotion and was told to plan to move into his new office the following Monday. It wasn't until Eric began packing his things that he started to feel some doubt about his seeming good fortune. Over the next few days, Eric became increasingly anxious about the implications of his new role. He thought it a bit strange that he should be worried about an opportunity such as this and decided his feelings must just be the typical cold feet over a new assignment.

Eric arrived at his new office on Monday morning ready for his new role, although he wasn't precisely sure what it would be. After meeting with his secretary, he had an extended meeting with the vice president he reported to. It was at that meeting that Eric began to realize that he might have some difficulty with his new assignment. At the meeting his new boss launched into a discussion of the importance of Eric's new job. "Your job," he said, "is pivotal to the success of the organization. You must develop a keen understanding of interpersonal conflict, organizational politics, and the art of negotiation. The only way this department is going to thrive is if the people in it get along with each other and with those in other departments that they interface with regularly. The key," he went on, "is having the patience to listen to everyone's concerns, find the common ground between them, and bridge the gaps."

When his new boss left the room, Eric's heart sank. He knew that he lacked all the skills the vice president had talked about. What's more, he knew in his heart of hearts that he was the wrong person for the job. He had no patience for people who didn't see things his way and no desire to develop the ability to put himself in someone else's shoes.

Over the next few months, Eric's worst fears were realized. His new job was full of interpersonal gray areas. He spent most of his time trying to get other engineers off each other's backs and other departments off his back. Each day he grew increasingly impatient with other people's inability and unwillingness to see things his way. After about six weeks, he decided he could no longer handle the job and turned in his resignation.

While Eric was in a difficult situation, he could have avoided much of his trouble if he had not made one fatal assumption that most people make—that up is always the best way to go.

Prognosis

To survive this dilemma, you have to be introspective, honest with yourself, and somewhat bold in your career management. If you're willing to take a careful look at your position in your organization, you can often predict potential danger points in your progression before you are confronted with a decision. If you insist in believing that up is the only way to go, you're a sitting duck for the sort of bind Eric found himself in. If you believe that it's worth your energy to scrutinize any move, including a promotion, chances are good that you can avoid making upwardly mobile mistakes.

Prescription

Gaining clarity about what aspects of your current job match what you do well and those that are more difficult and less appealing will give you a good base from which to assess the potential dissatisfaction that might accompany a promotion. The first thing you need to do, once you're clear on what is and isn't working, is to look at the potential promotion to see if it involves more of the good stuff and less of the bad. Quite simply, a good promotion is one that enables you to do more of the things you do well and enjoy doing and less of what you do poorly and dislike. While there are times you might choose to take a position because of its potential, even though it doesn't thrill you, you have to be careful that you don't end up on the wrong career path. If you rush the decision, you might find yourself traveling down a dead-end street, or worse, like Eric, going down the wrong street.

Once you've determined whether a potential promotion is appropriate to your career plans, you need to develop a strategy before you are faced with the opportunity. Depending on your ability to make a decision once an offer occurs is dangerous because you can get swept away by the flattery and the trappings of the change. Forethought on this is also helpful because often you can guide your superiors away from making inappropriate plans for you and influence them in desirable directions.

Taking charge of the situation so that you don't end up with an undesirable promotion is a control issue. You must decide who is in control of your career. As I've said before, if you don't have a plan for yourself, chances are you will become part of someone else's plan, and the likelihood of your being satisfied with other people's plans for you is slim. You will reap the greatest satisfaction from having a clear sense of where you do and don't want to go and making decisions accordingly. When others in your organization, most likely superiors, are in control of your career, you run the risk of finding yourself part of an undesirable plan, one that can easily lead you astray.

Those running organizations are increasingly aware of the fact that in order to keep people they have to keep them happy. In unprecedented numbers, employees are refusing to be transferred geographically, are turning down promotions, and are making life-style decisions around work that would be heresy to the organization man of the 1950s and 1960s. If you look at the progression of this shift in terms of decades, it can offer an enlightening perspective. As the volatile social upheaval of the 1960s came to an end, most observers agree that working America entered two decades of achievement-oriented, acquisitive patterns. Beginning in the early 1970s, there were signs that "more is better" would be the rallying cry for a generation of working professionals. By the early 1980s the moniker "yuppie" would institutionalize that notion. Early rumblings suggest that the 1990s will signal yet another shift. BMW ads that exalt the virtues of "the ultimate driving machine" are being replaced by Toyota Tercel ads that talk about "the new values of quality and economy" as symbols of how things are changing. In the August 27, 1990, issue of *Fortune* magazine, the cover story on 25-year-olds proclaimed, "Today's managers are nothing like yuppies." Inside, the article presented numerous stories of people who were making other life-style considerations priority over career advancement. In case after case the baby busters (children of the baby boomers) chose things like "living a healthy life, less stress, and happiness and fulfillment" over promotions and fancy titles.

What this is saying to any executive who is paying attention is that the rules are changing and that management needs to start taking into account the shifted values that are the impetus for the new breed's career decision making. What this is saying to you is that it's okay to say no to a promotion for the right reasons. As long as you have good reasons for saying no and can articulate them, there's no reason to fear the repercussions of passing on a promotion. In fact, if you have an alternate plan for yourself, one that matches some need of the company, this is the perfect time to let your superiors know what that is. Turning down a promotion because there's something else that needs to be done that you are genuinely compelled to do will raise your esteem in the eyes of those who are most invested in seeing you and your company succeed.

IF YOU FIND YOURSELF GOING THE WRONG WAY ON THE COMPANY LADDER

Symptoms

This problem is the opposite of the promotion dilemma in that the organization is making a decision that you have no say in. The most distinct symptom of this condition is the uncomfortable sensation of moving down the steps of whatever career ladder you've been on in the company. Finding yourself facing a demotion is cause for concern and requires careful consideration on your part.

Diagnosis

This dilemma may or may not be obvious to you. In its obvious form, you experience a change in title, a change in duties, and perhaps even a cut in pay. In its less obvious form, you find yourself with a decrease in your level of responsibility, diminished opportunity, and perhaps even less to do. Your descent down the company ladder can be very fast or subtle and slow. In any event you need to evaluate your condition carefully and take appropriate action. Quite often such a descent means it's time to clean out your drawers and look for greener pastures; however, on occasion the shift may simply mean that you and/or your organization made a mistake and that the adjustment is getting you back to where you belong (for now).

Prognosis

If your downward movement is clearly an undesirable shift, it may very well be that your best move is out the door. If, however, you feel relieved and reprieved from a promotion that turned out to be a bad decision, it may be that your company is concerned about your success and is determined not to set you up for failure. If you feel you were given the wrong promotion and you can undo the damage without losing face or future opportunity within the organization, you may want to consider staying on.

Prescription

The first thing you need to do is to assess the career impact of your downward movement. If the shift feels like backpedaling and reflects a clear lack of progress, you need to find out what's behind it. Talking to your superiors about your condition will quickly give you a clear idea of whether you have an unsurmountable problem within the organization. Too many people leave the situation to unnecessary guesswork. Important to remember is that people can't help giving themselves away in this situation. Thinly veiled comments by superiors like "We feel this move is in your best interest" or "Around here we feel it's important to match people up realistically with their level of competence" suggest that you don't have the confidence of management that you need to thrive, and you'd better pack your bags.

If you've got management's good faith, as evidenced by such comments as "Let's talk about what's going on for you and figure out the best place for you so that we can really tap your potential," it may be that your stalled progress is temporary. If you hang in there, you may soon find yourself on a more appropriate track within the organization.

In any case, there's no point in being coy about the matter. Too many people think that by not talking about what's going on they are protecting themselves. In fact, quite the opposite is true. When you play games with the ladder, you may very well find yourself down the chute.

WHEN LOVE AND LABOR CROSS PATHS: THE DANGER OF MIXING INTIMACY AND WORK

Symptoms

No dilemma is more potentially volatile than handling sexual politics in the workplace. You're faced with this when you find yourself feeling strongly about someone at work and those feelings go beyond a sense of camaraderie from working well together. Preoccupation with another person's comings and goings, fantasizing about a nonexistent relationship, and romanticizing a person's otherwise casual responses to you are all signs that you might be falling for someone at work. If you find yourself thinking more about this person than you do about your work, you know you've got this bug. The longer it goes unaddressed, the more difficult this problem will be to remedy.

Diagnosis

In fact, this may or may not be a problem. "Romance at work" books are full of happy endings for stories of falling in love at work. However, there are several factors that determine whether the situation is a problem or an opportunity. It can be an opportunity if you and the object of your affection are not already committed, that is, married. It is also important that the organization you're in has a high tolerance for such situations. If it doesn't, you could find yourself gaining a lover and losing a job—a choice not to be made hastily.

If you find yourself smitten with someone who is already taken or you are in an organization that frowns on mixing love and labor, then you'd better be prepared to make some hard decisions.

Prognosis

Many people believe that in this career-conscious age, the best place to find a mate is at work. If the conditions outlined in the diagnosis are favorable and the obstacles absent, then your romance has a reasonable chance of survival. If you face serious obstacles, such as one of you is already married or your employer is intolerant, your chances of emerging unscathed, unless you nip it in the bud, are slim.

Prescription

This prescription, like many, varies depending on the nature of the problem. If the person you've chosen is unattainable or the environment hostile to such liaisons, my advice is to do everything you can to get unhooked. This may mean seeking therapy, getting reassigned, or even leaving the organization. The last thing you want is to find yourself pining for someone you can't have and sacrificing your dignity and the quality of your work in the process.

If you find yourself attracted to someone at work, the attraction is mutual, *and* the other person is unattached, proceed carefully. Know that everyone around you probably knows something is going on and will be watching. Even if the organization tolerates such activity, people will be concerned that budding relationships might turn into nepotism. The best way to handle this is to be as public about it as is comfortable. People hide these things only when they think there is something wrong with what they are doing. Going public may be hard to do, particularly if you are a private person, but it ultimately makes the most sense. If your relationship remains secretive, people will use secrets against you. If there are no secrets, you've disarmed your potential enemies. Turning a workplace relationship into a viable solid personal relationship is tricky at best, yet it can be done. Be sure before proceeding that the conditions are right for the relationship to succeed, that there are no major obstacles, and, most important, that the person is worth it.

MOMMY TRACKS, BACKWATER FLATS, AND OTHER PIGEONHOLES

In the first chapter I talked about concepts like midlife crisis, burnout, and workaholism, suggesting they were misnomers for deeper, more complex problems. This section deals with occupational pigeonholing which can be equally misleading. The danger comes from being placed in one of these boxes, which limits others' view of what you have to offer.

Symptoms

Other than the obvious "She's on the mommy track" or " He works in the backwater," the way to tell if you're being inappropriately pigeonholed is if you find people treating you in a way that limits your performance. The danger here is that the pigeonholing will limit people's expectations of you in a way that could slow your progress.

Diagnosis

Pigeonholes can be distinct, as in the mommy track, or vague and general, as in reference to the corporate backwater. The notion of the mommy track suggests that performance expectations for childbearing women are different than those for other women. Felice Schwartz, of Catalyst, who first suggested the notion (but never used the term) in an article in the *Harvard Business Review*, received a great deal of flak from feminists who saw her position as one that would "set back the clock" on women's progress. While Schwartz maintains that her original article was prowoman and misunderstood by her detractors, the mommy track has established itself, as most catchy clichés do, as a label to be avoided. If you find yourself in an organization that views your motherhood as a limitation and narrows the range of opportunities available to you because of it, you either need to do something about it or change organizations (unless, of course, you like the limits placed on you as a result of your being a parent).

Being identified as someone who works in the corporate backwater can greatly limit your options in an organization. In this case, the backwater refers to departments that are not considered central to the purpose and goals of the organization. In some organizations, human resources is considered the backwater; in others, it's accounting or quality assurance or public relations. Regardless of what functions it refers to in a particular organization, if you're a resident of a backwater flat, you may find that your work is less valued and your prospects less bright than those in the more esteemed, "value-added" departments.

Prognosis

The greatest threat from this phenomenon is avoidance. People don't like to be pigeonholed and will quite often deny that it is happening to them. A careful, deliberate strategy can often save you from these sorts of traps, but you have to be willing to see the writing on the wall and do something about it.

Prescription

If you've been unwillingly placed on the mommy track, you need to do all you can to adjust your organization's viewpoint and remove the limitations such tracking can cause. Any pigeonholing that says that you cannot handle a maximum load greatly limits your potential in any thriving organization. Whether or not you have life-style considerations that limit your participation, you want to be careful to avoid any assumptions about your potential for involvement. The best way to deal with challenges that might create problems for you is on a case-by-case basis. Regardless of whether you are willing to take any and all assignments your company sends your way, you want to be the one to say no. The last thing you want is an institutionalized policy that limits your access to opportunity. If you suspect that such a policy exists, either formally or in the minds of those who matter, do your best to let those in power know that you have not placed any limits on yourself and that you hope that they would consider you for any and all projects that might match your talents.

If you find yourself pigeonholed in the backwater of your organization, there are several things you can do. You can develop the skills and strategy to market yourself internally into another department that is more highly regarded in the organization, you can move to another organization that places a greater value on what you do, or you can choose to champion your cause and turn your backwater flat into a high-class joint. What you do depends on how much you value your current work and your current organization. If you're tired of being treated like a second-class citizen and you believe that the reason is the line of work you've chosen, it's time to retool and redirect your career. If your backwater status is more closely linked to this particular organization than to your area of specialization, it's time to move on to an organization that values your skills more highly. Consider the possibility of making a move into a firm that specializes in providing the services you offer to other companies. If you do some investigating, you may find that one person's backwater flat is another's beachfront estate.

Your last alternative is to be a hero and raise the status of your humble department. While at first glance this may be the least appealing option, it can, if the conditions are right, lead to the greatest payoff. I know of one man who worked in the computer industry. His company was in trouble and, as is often the case, his department, human resources, took the biggest blow when it came time for restructuring. He watched as his department shrank from 30 professionals to five. As it was always considered the backwater of the organization, no one was surprised by the cuts. While everyone else scattered, looking for other work, this man decided that he really wanted to stay in the company and salvage what was left of what he believed was a critical part of the company's infrastructure. He held on through the hard times and managed to become head of the leaner, meaner department. As the company got back on its feet, it began hiring more people and had an increased need for—you guessed it—human resource development. Rather than refill old positions and recreate the backwater, the company, on the advice of our story's hero, decided to meet its human resource needs with consultants on an as-needed basis. This former captain of the backwater is now vice president of human resources, travels around the country scouting and hiring the best consultants, and meets regularly with the CEO to strategize about the company's future direction.

The point is that there are enough barriers to success out there. You don't need an additional stereotype placed on you that limits your potential. Whatever path you take, and whatever you decide to do, make your path unique and do the best job possible, and you'll be less likely to fall prey to these kinds of limitations.

ENEMIES IN THE OFFICE AND HOW TO HANDLE THEM

Symptoms

This is a highly charged topic, one that many people would just as soon avoid. Ideally, in the work environment people are committed to working together toward a common end. In the best of all possible worlds, one's work would be separate from one's personality, and the basis for success would be purely performance. Unfortunately, most work environments are fraught with conflicts between people. While you're better off avoiding creating enemies at all, there may be times you find yourself in the career-threatening situation of being enemies with a co-worker. You know you're in this situation when you have the distinct feeling that someone is out to get you, is sabotaging your work, or is soiling your reputation.

Diagnosis

Those people most turned off by the idea of enemies at work are in the most danger of being adversely affected by one. Dealing with someone who has set out to do you harm requires clear, intentional action on your part. What you need to do is determine the source of the hostility, the cause of it, and the forces driving the person's attack.

Prognosis

Enemies can be your undoing at work and create severe career damage if you don't take care of the situation. However, it's important to remember that more often than not people who create and thrive on enemy relationships at work often prove to be their own worst enemies. If you pay attention to the behavior of these combative types, you can usually develop a strategy that will work effectively against their attempts to cause you harm.

Prescription

One of the best ways to clarify this problem and determine a course of action is to focus on the situation rather than the person involved. Focusing on the person will distort your perspective and direct your energies toward something very difficult to change—someone's personality. Focusing on the situation will help you determine the best course to take to diffuse the conflict. By looking at an enemy situation as a conflict to be resolved, you simplify the matter and will be less likely to fuel the enemy fires and fall prey to your adversary's plans.

Most enemies fall into one of three categories: performance enemies, personal enemies, and political enemies. Performance enemies are at odds with your perfomance goals in the organization. Their source of discontent with you is that they don't agree with your plans, strategies, or goals within the parameters of your work. This is perhaps the easiest type of enemy to deal with because the problem is straightforward— you disagree on a desired outcome or the route for arriving at that outcome. The best way to deal with this sort of enemy situation is to confront the problem head-on. If you can, figure out what this person's objections are and, if it seems reasonable to you, modify your plans to diminish the disharmony. While this may not be your inclination when faced with an enemy— most people's first instinct is to fight back—you'll be amazed at the disarming affect your cooperation will have on your enemy's combativeness. "It takes two to tango" makes sense here. It's very difficult to fight with someone who won't fight back. If the changes required to defuse the tension are changes you can live with, surprise your performance enemies by complying with their desires and watch their rancor fade before your very eyes.

Personal enemies at work are far more difficult to handle because the problem is more intimate and more complex. If you believe people are out to cause you harm because of how they feel about you as a person, chances are the situation will not be easily alleviated. Several things are at stake here. A personal enemy at work can cause tremendous disruptions in your productivity and the productivity of those around you. They can also cause tremendous emotional drain. Finding yourself working with or around someone who obviously dislikes you will diminish your capacity to feel good about your work and do it well, and it can ultimately cause harm to your self-esteem.

The first thing to do is to determine whether the animosity

stems from something you've done or is related to something about you that is unchangeable. If you've done something to cause the animosity, you may want to consider undoing it by apologizing or offering some other sort of peace gesture. As with the performance enemy, the other party is apt to be surprised and caught off guard by your refusal to fight. Your gracious gesture could very well defuse the tension and get you out from under the emotional clutches that enemies can create.

If the source of the problem is something you are unable or unwilling to change, your choices are fewer. Say this person doesn't like your shortness, tallness, the way you dress, or some other factor that you can't or won't change. In this case you have a situation with limited options. Your best bet is to avoid such people as much as possible. If you can't, you may need to confront them about their bias. Since you can't or won't change your position, what's left is to change theirs. If they know their negative response to you is unacceptable and you're forceful enough about your objections, chances are good that they will stop responding negatively to you to your face— and that's half the battle.

The next thing you need to watch for is negative campaigning against you behind your back. In this situation the best way to respond is not to allow their covert activities to remain secret. If you have to, confront them and make them accountable for their actions in public. This way they will know—and everyone else will know—that their responses to you are unacceptable. Make your lack of tolerance of their negativity known as strongly and as loudly as possible; unless they're real warmongers, they'll leave you alone.

Political enemies can be difficult to detect because the animosity is based on your alliances with opposing forces. This is often the least personal type of enemy, yet they can cause serious damage because of the potential for loss. Because of the political nature of organizations, most people are forced into political alliances on a regular basis. When you take a position on any issue, you run the risk of creating political enemies. While this is often inevitable, the best thing you can do to limit this situation's impact on your career is to keep the conflict in perspective. If you find that someone you deem important to your career is on the other side of the political fence, do what you can to limit the polarization between the two of you. If you're not careful, a political enemy can turn into a personal and performance enemy as well. A little care can avoid such a scenario. If your relationship with this person was comfortable before the political conflict emerged, the best thing to do is have a candid conversation about the awkwardness of being on opposite sides of the fence. If you can establish that your differences are limited to the issue at hand and are not personal or performance based, you're likely to find that the situation is temporary and will not cause either of you long-term damage. Keep in mind that political positions should not be taken lightly. If you lose enough political battles, you may find yourself the object of a group of enemies, and when it comes to political enemies, groups can be far more powerful than individuals. The best way to avoid such a situation is to remain as independent as possible and not align yourself with any one group all the time. If you remain autonomous and flexible in your political positioning, you'll find that you're very much like the moving target that's far more difficult to hit.

TO GRIEVE OR NOT TO GRIEVE

Symptoms

Finding yourself the victim of an unfair or illegal act raises the question of whether you should file a grievance against your organization.

Diagnosis

The filing of a grievance is one of the more serious threats to your career and should never be taken lightly. However, there are times when the circumstances, your own values, or your need to protect yourself require you to enter the politically volatile arena of the grievance process. Before you choose to grieve, you should carefully weigh the pluses and minuses of your actions, your potential for succeeding, your alternatives, and the impact of the outcome on your future.

Prognosis

The political climate around employment issues and employee rights is so volatile that you should never assume you've got a surefire case. Many complainants have found themselves out in the cold from surefire cases that backfired. If your rights have been violated and you've got the proof, have tried every other alternative, and believe you can recover from any stigma attached to being a "griever," you may want to go ahead with formally filing a complaint.

Prescription

As is probably obvious from the prognosis, I believe that grievance procedures are most often too risky to be worth pursuing. However, in fairness to those of you who feel compelled to grieve an injustice caused you, I will review the conditions under which I think a grievance might make sense. But first, I will discuss alternatives to grievances that I think are far more productive.

If you believe you've been unfairly treated, your first move should be to confront the person you believe responsible for the unfair treatment. State your case and allow the other person an opportunity to correct the situation. If this is unsuccessful, you may want to consider going over this person's head to see if you can get the response you're looking for. If you think you might get the attention of those higher up in the organization, you could find yourself with a new job in the organization—one that bypasses the impact of your cause for grieving.

Be aware, however, that more than likely this sort of maneuver will not get you what you want. If you take this tack, you should be prepared to leave the organization once you've chosen to go over your boss's head. Another alternative before lodging a formal complaint is to consider the possibility of tapping into your organization's networks. If there's a group, either formal or informal, that has some power and influence, you may want to pursue your complaint through those channels to see if there's anything that can be done.

If you've explored these options and still feel you've been unfairly treated and have not received a satisfactory response, you have four choices: you can stay in the organization and accept their actions, you can stay and fight, you can walk away from the situation, or you can leave and fight. Each of the alternatives has a plus side and a minus side. If you stay and accept the actions levied against you, chances are your work will be the least disrupted by the condition that caused you to grieve. It is important to consider the impact the perpetrator's actions will have on your future, your feelings about what has happened, and your ability to live with the results. If you can accept that you've been treated unfairly, but you still like the work you do and your potential and can live with the decision, you may choose to let the inequity pass and let its impact fade with time.

Some people decide, for moral, ethical, political, or personal reasons, to stay in the organization and fight. This is probably the most difficult of the four choices. When you choose to lodge a formal complaint against your organization, it is essentially comparable to an act of war. By attempting to find your organization guilty of a criminal, immoral, or unethical act, you place yourself in an adversarial relationship with the organization that will probably never be undone. Even if you win the case, chances are that feelings will linger about your actions long after the actual case is resolved. I am not suggesting that you shouldn't do this. Such decisions are personal, private, and not subject to prescription. What I am suggesting is that you realize that you are forever changing your relationship to this organization. You need to accept that fact when you choose to proceed with a grievance or you will be in for a shock when the process is complete and you wait for things to "get back to normal."

Provided you can live with the decision, probably the easiest way to handle a situation in which you've been unfairly treated is to leave the organization and find another one that is more respectful of your rights and appreciative of your assets. The important thing about making this decision is being sure that you don't feel you are compromising your standards and making a decison that you feel uncomfortable with.

The fourth alternative is to leave the organization but not leave the grievance. This is probably the choice that will lead you to feel the most powerful. With this decision you leave the circumstances that were the source of your discontent, but you continue to make those who have wronged you accountable for their actions. If your level of comfort in your work environment is important to you, but your principles in relationship to the grievance are also important, this may be the preferred choice. The advantage is that you remove yourself from the tense situation, yet maintain your commitment to undoing the wrong that was done. The disadvantage is that you may find it difficult to make a move. People in the career marketplace get nervous when they find out you are the complainant in a grievance. Their initial reaction is, "What's it going to take to get them to grieve against *me*?" You need to realize this and be prepared to combat the image of you as a potential employee who is a troublemaker. If you can find a way to present your situation that diminishes people's focus on your grieving and emphasizes your cooperative and competent sides, you'll decrease the chances that being the defender of justice will work against you. However, you need to be keenly aware that if you take this tack there will be people who will hold your grievance against you no matter what you do.

It is important to keep in mind that the choice of whether to grieve is a very complex, personal one, that should not be made until you have examined all the possible outcomes and possibilities. When all is said and done, my advice is to grieve sparingly, hesitantly, carefully, and, if possible, not at all.

BEING ASKED TO DO SOMETHING ILLEGAL

Symptoms

Finding yourself in the unenviable position of being asked to do something that violates the law most often feels like you've been placed in a no-win situation with no apparent out. A distinct feeling of being trapped usually accompanies this condition.

Diagnosis

This can be a complicated decision that requires a careful assessment of the conditions surrounding the request. While it's clear to me that violating the law at the request of your employer is an unwise move, what is less clear, once you've decided not to comply, is what you do for your next move. Whether you take any action beyond noncompliance is the real question behind this dilemma and whether it gets in the way of your career.

Prognosis

There are many conditions under which this malady may occur. There are times when the request involves an inadvertent violation of the law, times when the violation is blatant, and times when there is an abundance of gray to wade through. Your employer's intention makes a tremendous difference here. If the request is a blatant effort to excel through compromising your integrity, then chances are slim that you can salvage the situation. If, however, the prospect of illegality is of a questionable nature, there may be ways you can bring this to your employer's attention. In this case your noncompliance may not hurt your career and may in fact help it.

Prescription

This is perhaps the trickiest political problem you can face in your career. While being asked to do something illegal may be cause for indignation, taking a superior attitude about the situation may only blind you to reality. If you believe a request is a blatant, intentional effort to get you to do something illegal for the benefit of the organization, your best bet is to refuse and accept whatever consequences may follow. Once you comply, you essentially become an accomplice. Just because your actions were condoned by your employer, don't think you'll be protected. If you doubt what I'm saying, consider the case of Michael Milken, creator of the junk bond. While his firm, Drexel, Burnham, Lambert, signed off on and, some suggest, choreographed his actions, Milken was the one ultimately found accountable for his actions by the courts. The firm ended up going under, but Milken ended up with the jail sentence. One can only guess at the impact on the firm, the stock market, and the American economy had Milken suggested to the firm that his plans might be lacking in propriety. Had he proposed a different course and had they listened, things might have worked out differently for everyone.

While there are times when your response to a request to act illegally is clear, there are other times when the choice is not so clear. There may very well be a time when the illegality requested is inadvertent. Treating an inadvertent mistake as an intentional illegal act can cause both you and your employer unnecessary hardship. Consider the case of George Bailey in the classic film *It's a Wonderful Life* as an example. In the story, George as a young boy works for a pharmacist. The pharmacist is filling a prescription for an elderly woman just after he receives news that his son has been declared missing in action overseas. He inadvertently fills the prescription capsules with poison and instructs George to deliver them. George attempts to inform his boss of the mistake, but the pharmacist, overcome by grief, fails to respond. George has a choice to make. He can fulfill his duties, deliver the poison, turn his boss in, and have him charged with attempted murder; or he can hold onto the capsules until he can get his boss's attention and rectify the situation. George makes the prudent choice and holds onto the capsules until he can convince his boss that he's made a mistake. The result is that his boss is saved from making a heinous error, the woman gets the right prescription, and, most important for this discussion, the pharmacist becomes forever indebted to George for saving the situation. In fact, we see later in the film that George and the pharmacist develop a lifelong relationship based largely on that one experience. If you've seen the film, you'll recall that in the fantasy sequence in which the story unfolds as though George's life never existed, the pharmacist makes the mistake, the patient dies, and the druggist's error leads him to life imprisonment.

The point is that there are times when you may be faced with a potentially illegal request that in fact is unintentional. You then have a choice that can make all the difference. You can participate in the illegal act and face grave consequences, you can refuse to participate and alienate your employer, or you can assess the situation to see if there is a way to prevent the illegal action and save—and perhaps even strengthen—your relationship with your employer in the process.

FIVE

Changes in Your Job that Can Hurt Your Career

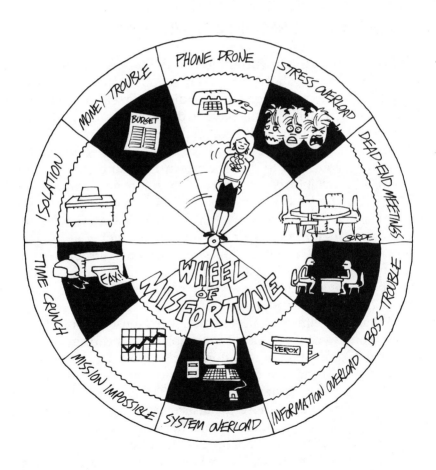

Many people make the mistake of thinking that the words "job" and "career" are synonymous. The problem with this is that it limits the potential of your career direction. A much better approach is to consider that your current job represents one phase of your career. That way you're much more likely to see your career existing on a continuum, subject to an infinite range of changes, rather than as something static that limits your opportunities.

THE PICTURE OF HEALTH: JOB WELLNESS

While looking at your current job as all there is to your career limits your potential, the reality is that your current work is the center of your career, for now. Finding yourself in a situation that is overwhelming can have a devastating effect on your career management and your sense of self-worth. Even if you're unhappy with your work and are committed to making a change, you need to do all you can to ensure that you are doing a good job in your current position and reaping the benefits that a productive work life has to offer. Job wellness exists when you have made an accurate assessment of the requirements for success on the job and are doing at least an adequate job of meeting those requirements. Problems like information overload, skill obsolescence, stress, unreasonable performance expectations, and poor time management can all sabotage your job wellness.

When job wellness is present, you feel a sense of control over your work. Even if you're not in the job of your choice, you feel the satisfaction of a job well done and can use your success to fuel your performance and, if necessary, to help you make a move in a more desirable direction. The problem for many people, particularly those disheartened with their current work, is that they underestimate the importance of current performance to future success. I see this often when I'm working with career changers. To some extent, it's understandable. If you've made a decision to change careers, that decision can often result in decreased commitment to your current work. The problem is that the decreased commitment can lead to diminished performance, which often leads to diminished self-esteem. It's hard to feel good about yourself at work when you know your performance is substandard. This diminished performance has a spiraling effect downward, and the impact on your future can be devastating. Consider the following scenario: You're a high school teacher who's decided to make a career shift to corporate training. You've done your homework and understand what it takes to make the transition. You've spent the last six months studying the corporate culture you're trying to enter, building your network, and preparing your paperwork so that you accurately present the skills you have that are transferrable from your current arena into your new one. The only problem is that in doing all this you've let your performance in the classroom slide. Your principal has noticed your lack of interest, your students have noticed your lack of involvement, and, worst of all, you have noticed your lack of effectiveness. You essentially feel like you're biding your time and performing at a minimum level until you can make the change and get the work you really want.

As a result your students' resentment builds, your principal's disappointment grows, and your sense of self-confidence diminishes. Eventually all your career search preparation pays off and you get a hot prospect. The problem is that you may enter the interview demoralized from your students' negative responses to you, you answer questions about your performance with a fair amount of self-doubt stemming from your current poor performance, and you get a mediocre recommendation from your disillusioned principal. You find yourself without a job offer and forced to continue working in a job that has become a nightmare for all involved.

The way to avoid this scenario is to focus on job wellness at all times—even when you're on your way out of a job or changing careers. This can be difficult to do because the usual instinct when moving out of a situation is toward diminished performance. As you can see from the previous scenario, this can backfire and lead to a prolonged stay in the job you're trying to get out of. Keep in mind that maintaining high job performance at all times will lead to increased career wellness *and* enhanced job mobility.

HANDLING INFORMATION OVERLOAD BEFORE IT HANDLES YOU

Symptoms

Finding yourself overwhelmed with the abundance of information coming your way and feeling a sense of powerlessness over that material are signs that you could be suffering from information overload.

Diagnosis

Ever since the computer became a fixture in the American workplace, the threat of information overload has been acute. The technology of the information age has spawned an unprecedented information explosion in just about every field. Instant access to information has led to a rise in performance expectations in just about every profession. Add to this information glut the proliferation of specialty magazines, journals, newsletters, reports, and increased book publications in every discipline, and it's easy to see how the average worker can become overwhelmed and even paralyzed by the amount and nature of available information. Try to keep up with every development in your field, and you're bound to find yourself drowning in paper.

Prognosis

Information overload is conquerable; however, what is required is a change in behavior. If you can learn to recognize and sort the essential from the peripheral, you can stay afloat.

Prescription

The first thing you need to do is realize that generating and disseminating information has itself become a discipline—one whose proponents base their success on your finding their work important. In essence, you are the object of the information generators' marketing blitz. Their success is dependent on your believing their information is invaluable to you. Knowing this, what you need to do is develop a way to examine and assess the information you receive and its sources. Being able to judge whether to pay attention to a particular source of information will go a long way in mastering the information glut and avoiding information overload. Follow these simple guidelines, and you'll probably emerge triumphant:

- Do you really need to know this information to make your work more effective? If not, skip it.

- Is the source of this particular information you have in front of you the most concise source of this information? If not, where can you get your hands on the most concise version? Get it.

- Can someone who reports to you boil down the information into a more concise yet equally thorough version? If so, have them do it.

- Is there someone you know who's already examined this information and is willing and able to give you a thorough report on the important factors? If there is, ask.

Follow these simple guidelines and you'll find the information explosion a valuable tool for your work rather than an overwhelming obstacle to it.

IF YOUR SKILLS BECOME OBSOLETE

Symptoms

Finding yourself losing ground in your ability to do your work because of technical changes is a sign that you are approaching skill obsolescence. Finding yourself out of sync with colleagues who are adopting new ways of operating at work is another clear sign. Finding yourself unable to compete in the marketplace because of a gap in skills is the surest sign that you have fallen prey to the threat of obsolescence.

Diagnosis

Most important in diagnosing the causes of this condition is narrowing the source. Has a new technology been introduced, have new norms for performance been adopted, is there new knowledge available, or are there environmental changes that have demanded new responses to the way the work is done?

Prognosis

If you can anticipate changes early in their development and take action to ensure that you aren't left behind, there's a good chance, if you're at all suited to what you do, that you can avoid finding your skills obsolete.

Prescription

In today's dramatically accelerated work world, the prospect of skill obsolescence exists for everyone. First grade teachers who don't learn enough about computers to respond to the skill levels some students bring with them into the classroom, physicians who don't develop ways to access crucial information available to them through complex data bases, and executives who don't develop the ability to evaluate the feasibility of their plans through the use of high-tech problem-solving models run the risk of finding themselves less effective in their work.

The key to avoiding obsolescence is to keep a careful eye on developments in your field. If a new technology is being introduced, find a way to familiarize yourself with it. Don't wait until it becomes the accepted standard. Get involved as early and in as much depth as is possible, and you'll find not only that you are not obsolete but also that you are a sought-after member of your profession.

If you sense the dawn of new performance standards for your profession, get a handle on what they are and begin strategizing about ways you can meet and exceed those standards. If there are new breakthroughs in knowledge related to your field, do what you need to do to find out about those advances, including reading reports on them, attending seminars focused on them, and talking with colleagues about the implications of those changes on your work.

If there are changes occurring in the way your work is being done, examine what those changes suggest in terms of new skills. For example, if you're working for an organization that announces its plans to start functioning in new ways using high-performance teams instead of the traditional content-clustered work groups, ask yourself what you need to do to equip yourself to handle those changes. I know of one large insurance agency that's recently undergone a major reorganization. Instead of all the underwriters working together, all the cost analysts working together, and all the sales reps working together, workers have been divided up into teams consisting of one person from each specialty area. The idea behind it is that each team will have the know-how to do anything the customer wants without having to refer to other groups. What this has done is to create a situation where each manager (and everyone on the team is now a manager) has to be able to manage the team. The interesting thing is that some of the managers are handling the changes far better than others. Those who are succeeding recognized early in the process that they needed new skills in order to survive and thrive. They're the ones who immediately started taking courses and reading about such subjects as team building, group dynamics, and conflict management. The ones who did nothing to build the skills required by the new work environment have been left in the dust, fearing their newfound obsolescence will cost them their jobs.

In the contemporary work world, change is constant. Most observers of work in America will tell you that the key to remaining competitive in the global marketplace is the extent to which the workforce can adapt and shift to the ever-changing market demands. If you don't accept this reality, you run the risk of finding yourself obsolete—and it can happen with the blink of an eye.

WHEN THERE'S TOO MUCH STRESS FOR SUCCESS

Symptoms

The symptoms of too much stress on the job can take many forms. Finding yourself emotionally upset to the point where you can no longer perform your duties is a sign of distress. Finding yourself focusing all your psychic energy on problems rather than on productivity is a sign of distress. Finding your body unwilling to continue to function because of the pressure at work is a sure sign of distress.

Diagnosis

As the symptoms suggest, three types of stress can have a negative impact on your performance at work. Emotional, psychological, and physical distress are the three most likely indicators that your levels of stress have reached dysfunctional proportions.

Prognosis

Stress at work is neither good nor bad. It simply exists. If you're in a job that has no stress, you probably aren't being very productive, creative, or effective. You're probably not getting paid very much either. Work stress is a reality of organizational life. The key to handling stress at work is to develop strategies before you need them. If you wait until your emotions, your psyche, or your body is under siege, it's too late.

Prescription

Ten Ways to Master Stress at Work   You'll notice that this section does not refer to avoiding, reducing, or limiting stress. It intentionally refers to *mastering* stress. What makes the difference in whether stress helps you perform better at work or is your undoing at work is the extent to which you are able to master it. Here are ten things you can do to take and maintain control over stress at work.

1. **Find and Use Ways to Minimize Tension and Anxiety.** Tension and anxiety are realities in any dynamic work environment. While a certain nervous edge can be an effective motivator, there's a point beyond which sustained tension or anxiety ceases to be productive. Being able to recognize your tension threshold and relieve conditions before you're over the edge is key. To relieve the tension and anxiety that accompany a touchy work situation, you don't need to change the situation; instead, you need to change your perspective. There are many ways to do this.

   One of the most reasonable techniques, from my perspective, was developed by a man named Herbert Benson. It's called the "relaxation response." Benson studied the techniques used by Zen masters in their meditation and modified them to meet the requirements of the Western mind. The result was a simple, scientifically proven, fast way to reap the benefits of meditation without having to buy into the spiritual component associated with Buddhist practice. If you've ever been exposed to Transcendental Meditation, which was phenomenally popular in the 1960s and 1970s, you'll recognize the technique. The difference is that you don't need to participate in a religious ritual offering flowers and fruit in exchange for your mantra. All you need do is pick up Benson's book, *The Relaxation Response,* and practice the 20-minute technique twice a day. You'll experience less tension and anxiety, and the result will be an enhanced ability to handle stress on the job.

If meditation is not your modality, don't despair. There are many other ways to reduce tension and anxiety. For some it's a daily walk, for others it's listening to music, and for others it's reading a book (for pleasure, not work!) or regular quiet time. Be careful about your choices here. A recent study on television watching reported that the majority of subjects got up from watching television less relaxed than when they sat down. The important thing is that you find something to do that is not physically taxing and that allows your body and mind to rest. Full-court basketball or cross-country running can be great ways to keep in shape (I'll talk about that later), but they are no substitute for the psychic and physical rest you need to keep stress at bay. Whatever you decide to do to take time out, it's important that it be pleasurable, restful, and something you do at least every other day.

2. **Maintain Reasonable Performance Expectations for Yourself.**   In the age of superman and supermom, it is difficult to maintain reasonable performance expectations for yourself. However, nothing produces more stress than finding that there is no possible way for you to do all that you've set out to do. This tactic for mastering stress has to do with reality testing and reality adjusting. If you suspect you've carved out a more demanding niche than is humanly possible, you owe it to yourself to adjust your expectations. Nothing can be gained from setting goals that are unachievable. While you want to be sure, if you're ambitious, to stretch yourself beyond your present boundaries, if the tension you've set your stretching apparatus on is too demanding for your current capacity, you run the risk of snapping the muscles you're trying to stretch. If you're not careful, you will find yourself incapacitated for an extended period. My advice here is simple. If you find yourself constantly overloaded and playing catch-up all the time, you need to eliminate some of the

demands you've placed on yourself and give yourself a reasonable chance of achieving the goals that are most important to you.

3. **Watch Your Diet.**   If it's true that you are what you eat, then most of us are walking garbage receptacles. Seriously, one of the ways we set ourselves up for increased stress at work is through what we eat. I don't know about you, but I find that the more stressful things are, the worse my eating habits get. This can be difficult to turn around yet is critical if you find yourself experiencing significant levels of distress. While I have neither the knowledge nor the inclination to offer dietary advice here, I do know that the tendency to adopt and sustain poor dietary habits when stress accelerates is a fairly common phenomenon. What this does is add insult to injury. The next time you find yourself overstressed, head for the salad bar instead of the make-your-own-sundae bar, and you'll be doing yourself and your stress level a favor. Keep in mind that the more you maintain a diet that is healthy and offers you the energy and vitality that you need to perform your best, the more likely you are to maintain the upper hand in the battle to master stress.

4. **Develop and Use a Personal Fitness and Wellness Plan.** As with diet, taking measures to ensure your fitness will go a long way in mastering stress. Have a plan for maintaining a fit body, and it will serve your mind in countless ways when the stressors hit. Find ways of exercising regularly that do not require a great deal of effort. Some people find fitness equipment in their home or office is most convenient, others prefer the social setting of a health club, while others need the structure of a class to keep them motivated. Whatever your preference, the important thing is to build an exercise pattern into your routine so that your fitness activity is automatic and likely to continue during stressful times.

In addition, do what you need to do to maintain your overall wellness by monitoring changes in the way you feel and taking dietary supplements if needed. While you want to be careful to not overmedicate yourself, taking care of ailments that require relief is critical to your stress mastery. While you, like many people, may feel increasingly disillusioned with modern medicine, you need to be careful to attend to medical concerns. Trying to ignore a situation that needs diagnosis and treatment can cause high levels of distress that, combined with work stress, can take you over the edge. Whatever the concern, no matter how small or how big, get the answers you need for peace of mind, and your stress mastery will be heightened.

5. **Minimize Contact with People Who Drive You Crazy.** This may be difficult to do if the person in question is your boss, co-worker, or subordinate. In those cases you may have to deal with the problem in an in-depth way. What I'm talking about here is consciously avoiding people in your life who are avoidable. These may be people you see out of habit, people you've had prior involvement with, or people you feel an ongoing commitment to, like family. You should carefully monitor your contact with unnecessary stress inducers during particularly stressful times. If there are people at work, for example, who are chronic complainers and you are one of their standard sounding boards, you may want to drop out of the rotation during periods of significant stress. Chances are these people have other resources to draw on and will not miss your availability. In fact, you may be surprised at the extent to which some of these people will understand your need for distance during difficult times. Also, don't underestimate the impact that nonwork contacts can have on your stress levels at work. If you find you're entering a difficult period at work, let family and friends who you find challenging to be with know that you may be unavailable for a while. This may be difficult to do but in the long run can give you the breathing room you need until you're out from under the gun.

6. **Use Imagery and Visualization to Help You Handle Difficult Situations.** This is perhaps the most powerful tool you can have for minimizing the powerlessness you can

feel from extreme stress. My wife and I recently experienced the power of the technique in helping my six-year-old son overcome some particularly stressful dreams. We found some help from a wonderful book called *Nightmare Help* (Ten Speed Press, 1989) by Anne Sayre Wiseman. In the book Wiseman recommends helping children cope with bad dreams by giving them symbolic power over the threatening forces. One example she gives is of a child who is fearful of a beast. She describes how she instructs the child to draw a picture of the beast and then asks the child what he could do to make the beast less threatening. The child proceeds to draw bars around the beast until the monster is fully and safely enclosed in a cage.

In my son's case he was trying to deal with a particularly terrifying alien who had emerged from a cemetery. He drew a fairly gruesome picture of this creature and said that he found him extremely scary. I then asked him to draw a picture of himself on the same page as the alien. The picture he drew of himself was about a tenth the size of the one of the alien. I then asked him what he might do to make the alien less scary. He thought for a moment and then drew another picture of himself, this time ten times larger than the picture of the alien. I then asked him to write a message to the alien. He formed a cartoon bubble over his head and said to the alien, "Get lost, little guy." When I asked him how he felt now, he said he found the alien much less scary and suggested that he might go back to bed. I agreed and watched astounded as he fell into a deep and peaceful sleep that lasted through the night.

Now I'm not suggesting that you hang around your workplace drawing pictures of your stress monsters. What I am suggesting is that one of the most profound stressors at work is the perception that the problem you are facing is much larger than you and is likely to devour you. You don't need crayons and paper to shrink your monsters down to size; you can do it in your mind. Find ways to visualize problems in a way that makes you feel less powerless, and you will begin to feel relief almost instantly. Shift your perspective on the problem so that you are not the victim but rather the master of the situation, and you will begin to see alternatives that enable you to take action toward relieving the stress. If you can learn to perceive a seemingly overwhelming problem as simply a manageable inconvenience, you've won half the battle in conquering the stress monsters.

7. **Work in the "C" Zone.**   There are countless books on the subject of stress. You can take tests that will tell you how stressed you are at work or at home. You can find out what your chronic or circumstantial stress levels are and how you compare to the rest of the population. While some people find these indicators helpful, my experience in using them is that most people are off the charts. Besides, I think most people have a pretty good idea of whether or not they have too much stress for success. Of all the material out there on stress, there's one book I've found extremely valuable because of its simple and direct message for managing stress. It's called *The "C" Zone: Peak Performance under Pressure* by Robert and Marilyn Harris Kriegel (Fawcett Books, 1984). The "C" zone derives its name from prior theories on stress that you are probably familiar with, that is, type A and type B theories. Typically people who are type A are hard-driving, ambitious, extremely active, and overly stressed. Type B people are typically laid-back, relaxed, easygoing, and somewhat understressed. What the Kriegels found—and I agree—is that neither type fits the profile of a peak performer; thus they coined the term "C" zone.

People operating in the "C" zone demonstrate three consistent characteristics: they are in control, are confident, and have commitment to the task at hand. While most stress theorists expend energy talking about the merits and shortcomings of A types and B types, the message of the "C" zone is that the key to mastering stress is directly tied to your ability to control the situation that's causing you stress, your level of confidence in your ability to handle the situation, and your level of commitment to mastering the problem at hand. Focusing on the three Cs will do far more for you than spending your time worrying about whether you should be more or less of an A or a B.

8. **Develop Your Ability to Manage Conflicts.** One of the major sources of stress at work is conflict with co-workers. While I have discussed strategies for handling specific conflict situations throughout this book, I'd like to share a model that over the years I have found to serve as a template for assessing and responding to conflict situations. It's called the Thomas-Kilmann Conflict Mode Instrument by Kenneth Thomas and Ralph Kilmann. It first appeared in print in an article entitled "Conflict and Conflict Management" by Kenneth Thomas in volume 2 of *The Handbook of Industrial and Organizational Psychology,* edited by Marvin Dunnette (Chicago: Rand McNally, 1975).

The model suggests that there are five types of appropriate responses to conflict, depending on how assertive and how cooperative you want to be in any particular situation. The five responses are avoiding, accommodating, compromising, competing, and collaborating. The tack you take depends upon the extent to which you want to win and the extent to which you want the other person to win. If neither of you really cares about winning, you may choose to avoid the conflict entirely. If you percieve that the other person cares more than you do, you may choose to accommodate. If you want to win at any cost, you may choose to compete. If you want to arrive at a win-win outcome, you may want to collaborate. If you want win-win but collaboration seems unmanageable, you may choose to compromise. It's important to realize that compromise differs from collaboration in that with the latter both sides get what they want and in the former both sides give up some of what they want. While choosing among the five alternatives is more complex than this simple outline, I offer it to you as a frame of reference for choosing a strategy in a conflict situation. The important thing about mastering stress through effective conflict management is deciding what you need to get and what you are willing to give up and then acting accordingly.

9. **Find and Use Distractions.**   For many successful professionals, work becomes an obsession. There was a brief period in the mid-1970s when people were talking about the four-day workweek. In the 1980s, that notion lost ground and was replaced by the notion of the 60 to 70-hour workweek. In "Twelve Reasons for Leaving at Five" in *Fortune* magazine (July 19, 1990), Walter Kiechel III made a plea for the 40-hour workweek, suggesting that there are many work-related and other reasons for leaving the office at five o'clock. To the mass of professionals buying into the 70-hour workweek norm, the article must have sounded like a cry in the dark—one that they most likely echoed in the privacy of their own overstressed minds. Even though Kiechel and others report on studies that suggest people lose their productivity after eight hours, corporate downsizing and streamlining have led to increased time demands on everyone.

The challenge, from a stress mastery perspective, is to buck the trend. Enter into a psychological contract with your employer that says you can and will get the work done in the eight-hour day and then use your well-earned discretionary time to do things that you find distracting, entertaining, and, yes, heaven forbid, fun. The point is that when the going gets tough, the tough lose their sense of adventure. Even the most nose-to-the-grindstone professional needs time to forget about work and enjoy the simple—or extravagant—pleasures that refuel them and recharge them for the work at hand. Find and make the time to do the things that reenergize you; your work will improve, and your distress will diminish.

10. **Give Up the Quest for Control Over the Uncontrollable.**   One of the greatest stressors at work is the quest to control the uncontrollable. The futility of such activity is the true source of the stress. Twelve-step programs such as Alcoholics Anonymous know this well. Their basic tenet

about changing what is changeable, accepting what isn't, and knowing the difference can offer a perspective to the overstressed would-be controller that no amount of manipulation can match. Too many people think that they can get others to do what they would like simply by choreographing a set of responses to a situation. The problem is that some variables are inevitably out of your control. While it's true that you can sometimes change someone's behavior by reinforcing the behavior you would like to see, the chances of your changing someone's true nature are slim. Remember, the easiest person to change is yourself. Change your own responses to a situation, and you may see the results you want—or you may not. If you don't get someone to do what you want, you need to accept that there is nothing you can do about it. Dwelling on your lack of ability to influence someone in your direction will cause you undue stress.

Once you've given it your best shot and haven't gotten the results you want, leave it alone. Nothing is worse for your stress levels than trying to change the unchangeable. I run into this problem with job changers all the time. It sometimes takes days to debrief an applicant who came in second for a position and to get them off the self-defeating cycle of "what I should have done and could have done that I didn't do." Getting someone to leave the unchangeable behind and move on to the next possibility is a critical hurdle. It's the same reason I tell unemployed people not to read the unemployment statistics; there's nothing you can do about them, and all it does is add to the stress. The next time you're feeling overstressed about a situation, be sure to sort out the things you're worrying about that you can't control and the things you're worrying about that you can control. Get rid of the uncontrollables, and you'll most likely cut your stress in half.

As I mentioned earlier, my intent here is not to offer you a comprehensive treatise on managing stress. What I've tried to do is provide an overview of the key tactics I have found useful in harnessing and mastering this inescapable thing called stress.

Stress and the Job Search. The stress of the job search is so unique that it requires its own discussion. I've seen many highly competent professionals fall apart when it comes time to manage a job search. In light of the fact that one's livelihood and sense of security are at stake, this response is understandable. While all the strategies outlined in the previous section apply, there are some additional things you can do to make sure your stress meter doesn't stay in the red during your entire search.

In my first book, *CareerMap* (Wiley, 1988), I broke the job search process into five steps called the P.O.I.N.T. process: persuasive paperwork, occupational investigation, influential interviewing, networking, and tracking leads. Each of these critical steps can be handled in a way that either alleviates job search stress or exacerbates it.

1. **Persuasive Paperwork.** When doing resumes and cover letters for a job search, you need to honestly assess your writing skills. If you are a good writer and confident that your paperwork conveys what you want it to, spend some time with a good word processor developing a series of alternative resumes and letters to use for the various types of jobs you apply for. This is far less stressful than trying to write a custom resume and letter for each prospect that appears. If you've got an assortment of documents prewritten, all you need to do is pick the one most appropriate for the job in question and then customize it with a focused objective reflecting your goals in terms of the expressed interests of the potential employer.

   If you are less than confident about your writing skills, you need to find a good writer to help you develop these materials. Be careful not to pawn this uncomfortable but necessary task onto a professional resume writer. Chances are they will distort your material to the point where it is unrecognizable to you. What you need is someone with good writing skills who won't put words in your mouth but will help you get your words on paper in the most persuasive, effective way. Careful attention to your paperwork so that it's ready to fly at a moment's notice will alleviate the undue stress that resume and letter writing can create when you're faced with an application deadline.

2. **Occupational Investigation.** Investigating prospective fields, organizations, industries, and occupations is one of the cornerstones of an effective job search. The research or information interview long held by experts as a key to the effective search requires a certain amount of gregariousness. Some people, when faced with the prospect of approaching prospective employers to explore potential opportunities, eagerly embrace the notion and find the permission they've been granted to approach people as liberating; others become terrified at the thought. If you're one of those people who likes the thought of hitting on people cold to talk with them about your career, you need to temper your enthusiasm so that you don't turn them off. For example, lately I've had several people call me and say that they wanted to "tap my network," an approach I resent. If you're not sensitive in your approach, you'll soon be faced with the stress associated with wondering why information interviewing works for everyone but you.

If you're at the other end of the spectrum and are intimidated by the notion of talking to strangers about your career, you need to realize that there are ways to conduct research interviews without having to be a social Rambo. If the notion of information interviewing gives you cold sweats, there are two things you can do to make the situation less stressful. The first is to pick the perfect interviewee rather than the perfect stranger. Start with someone you know and trust will respond to you positively. Ask them for the interview, let them know that you're picking them because you're nervous and knew they would be a safe bet, and ask them to critique your performance once you're done. Do this with as many people as you need to until you're at the point where the perfect stranger feels like the next perfect interviewee. If you're still nervous about contacting people you don't know, start with the least threatening communication, a letter of introduction. Since this is a one-way communication, you can say exactly what you want to say without worrying about it coming out the wrong way. You can then make a follow-up phone call, an act much less threatening than a cold phone call. The crucial thing in all this is that you find ways to do the all-important investigating in a way that you find relatively nonthreatening; that way you don't avoid the act entirely and thus prolong your unemployment—which is the ultimate stressor.

3. **Influential Interviewing.**   When going on actual job interviews, do all you can to minimize your stress levels. Prepare as much as possible for the interview, go into the interview with as much confidence as possible, and accept that the only thing you have control over is your own performance. Focus on performing at your peak, be as enthusiastic and articulate as possible, and let all the factors over which you have no control take care of themselves.

4. **Networking.**   As mentioned in the occupational investigation section, don't assume that everyone you're interested in networking with is going to be interested in networking with you. Be respectful of other people's time and mindful of their boundaries, and you're far more likely to get what you want from others. Most important, don't underestimate the value of networking. It continues to be the number-one way people get work. A *USA Today* survey (November 1, 1990) reported that at a time when layoffs are soaring, 60 percent of job seekers are getting their jobs through networking.

There's another important aspect of networks that can have a significant impact on your stress levels. During the job search it's important that you have a network of people who support your search efforts. The tricky thing about this is that you may be surprised at the lack of support you get from your usual network. There are several reasons for this. Some of the people in your network, like your spouse and other people who are dependent on you, have a lot to lose or gain as a result of your search. It can be very difficult for them to put their own needs aside and give you the support you need. This is especially true if your job search was precipitated by a self-induced career change. Friends and colleagues may react unpredictably as well. Quite often a fellow worker who chooses to leave an organization creates a ripple effect that forces everyone else to confront their own dissatisfaction. It's similar to the impact a marital breakup has on a circle of friends—it shakes up the whole system and forces friends to look at the stability of their own situations.

For these reasons it's important that you surround yourself with people who sympathize and empathize with what you're going through. You may find these people in a career search course, a civic group, a Forty Plus club (which specializes in this sort of thing), or some other informal setting. The important thing to know for the sake of stress management is that you need to find people who support you in your efforts and that these people may not be part of your usual support network.

5. **Tracking Leads.** This step refers to following through on any hint of possibility in your job search and not just relying on the most likely possibilities. What this does for your stress level is significant because one of the most debilitating factors in your job search is the loss of hope. The philosophy behind lead tracking is that if you follow through on enough long shots, you can end up with a sure bet. By pursuing any and every lead, you maintain a sense of optimism that is a great contrast to the sense of dread from sitting at home and waiting for the phone to ring. Tracking leads not only reduces your stress levels but also can often pay off in the end as well.

Marty K.—Proof that Persistence Pays   I meet quite a few people who expend lots of energy talking about why they can't do what it is they want to do. I in turn expend a great deal of energy trying to convince them that they can do it. Occasionally I meet people who exemplify the power of aiming at a goal and are effective at tracking leads until they get what they want. Marty K. is one of those people.

From 1974 to 1986 Marty K. was a blacksmith specializing in making fireplace tools, eighteenth-century door hardware, iron railings, and various other objects as requested. "After twelve years I decided to make a change because my values shifted. I was tired of working alone, tired of being so hard on my body and I wanted to start using my head more than my hands."

I met Marty in 1986 when he approached me about the possibility of taking my Career Renewal workshop series. "I'm going to be a tough nut to crack," he said. After taking the course Marty entered what he described as a hellish year and a half. "During that period I applied for 50 positions in various fields. I had several close calls, but I continually had to confront employers who were unable to understand that I might have some transferrable skills.

"At one point I took a job with a local rose grower. Three days a week, at 3:00 in the morning, I drove a load of roses into a wholesale flower market in Boston, where I acted as a sales rep. Six months of that insane schedule was about all I could tolerate."

After sorting out all that had happened to him during this difficult time, Marty decided to focus his efforts on work in real estate. "I took a course to get my real estate license and applied for a job with a local residential agency. They gave me a battery of psychological tests and told me that while I scored high in intelligence they didn't think I had the personality to sell real estate." Marty didn't give up on the idea in spite of the negative feedback and eventually took a job as an apartment rental agent. While at this job he was asked to try his hand at commercial leasing, at which he was very successful. In 1987 he leased more commercial space than any other agent in his city.

When he was still self-described as a "medium-sized fish in a small pond," Marty received a call from a headhunter who was looking for "a heavy hitter" for a blue chip commercial firm in a nearby larger city. After an initial conversation, the headhunter felt that Marty did not have the experience he was looking for but suggested there was an outside chance that he could get him in for an interview. Marty pursued the possibility, an admitted long shot, and eventually got the interview and the job. He is currently working on a deal that, if successful, will be one of the largest sales of commercial property to happen in his city in a long time.

As I sit with Marty in his twentieth-floor office overlooking the Connecticut River, I'm struck by the sense of self-confidence he now projects. "It's been a long, hard journey from the forge to my office in the tower overlooking the river. I suppose there's something to be said for perseverance in the face of adversity and being open to change, even when you're not too clear about where you're headed."

I asked Marty where he's headed from here. "The commercial real estate market is in a real slump right now and things are tough. I might decide to move on. I don't know if I'll stay in real estate or pursue something else. I might go to the next level of certification in commercial real estate and stick with it. If you stay in this business long enough, you can do well and survive even during the hard times. Or I might decide to do something else. There are a couple of possibilities out there."

As I left his office, I was struck by Marty's ability to accept the uncertainty his future holds and convinced that whatever he decides to do he'll be able to convince someone to let him do it. He is persistent, he never gives up, and he is an expert at tracking leads.

WHEN TWO JOBS ARE NOT BETTER THAN ONE

Symptoms

The age of downsizing can be a boon to your career if you're one of the survivors of the shrinkage. However, if you're not careful, you can find yourself doing the work of two or more people—too much for any one career. Gaining additional responsibilities as the result of downsizing is not a problem in and of itself. Problems emerge when the nature of the shift in responsibility is such that your work now requires you to be in two places at once, doing two things at once, or filling two roles at once. While most people can handle this sort of split for a brief period, it can prove tremendously draining and defeating if it is a constant condition.

Diagnosis

What you need to figure out early in the game is whether feeling split and fragmented is a temporary condition caused by your lack of familiarity with the new dimensions of your role or whether it's the nature of the newly created position.

Prognosis

If the problem is a matter of integrating your new responsibilities with the old, all you need do is practice your juggling. If the new responsibilities offer you opportunities beyond those of your former ones, consider yourself fortunate to have been in the right place at the right time. If after careful examination, however, you realize that in no way is it humanly possible to do both jobs well, you need to act carefully and swiftly to prevent serious damage to your career.

Prescription

Wearing two hats on a permanent basis will leave you at a disadvantage compared with colleagues who are able to focus all their energies on one role. If you find your organization has saddled you with two horses to ride, you need to let them know that in order to remain effective they need to help you dismount one of them as soon as possible—preferably your less preferred one. It's important to remember that unless you let your concern be known it is unlikely that your organization will help you get out from under this problem. After all, it's attractive to downsizing management to think they can actually have one person do two jobs.

When approaching your superiors with your concern, make sure you have a plan, not just a complaint. Your success in rectifying the situation will be determined by your ability to offer them a solution to their problem at the same time that you retake control of your own situation. Take a look at the the two roles you're carrying. Figure out which one you value more and do better, and make a case for why that should be the one you keep. Also examine the role you're giving up and see if there's a way to eliminate it without losing key functions critical to the organization. You'll have a much easier time convincing management to eliminate a role than you will getting them to give it to someone else. If both roles are essential, you simply need to make it clear that in order to do one job optimally you need to cast off the other one. To support your case and remain positive in this difficult scenario, focus on what you plan to do in your remaining role that will benefit the organization. If management is at all reasonable, they will understand that your concerns are performance based, not avoidance based, and they'll do all they can to shift the excess load. If they're not reasonable, you might as well start looking for new work because eventually the two roles will be too much and you will end up the loser.

MISSION IMPOSSIBLE: HANDLING UNREASONABLE PERFORMANCE EXPECTATIONS

Symptoms

Most successful people like to think they can handle any challenge that comes their way. While it's great for your career to be a superstar, increased success brings increased expectations. Finding yourself the "fast-track water walker" in your organization can be a setup if you're not up to it—or if there's no way anyone could do what's been asked of you. Feeling that you've been asked to do the impossible is a sure sign that you're about to become the victim of your own success.

Diagnosis

The people most vulnerable to this condition are those whose superiors respond to their success by saying, "That's great, but what are you going to do for me tomorrow?" There are many signals when you're in a situation propelling you toward unrealistic performance expectations. If you get the feeling that everyone in your organization is beginning to see you as the most successful person around, it's great for your ego, but it can be a setup as well. Those around you may start seeing you as someone for whom success comes easily; if you're like many people who are good at what they do, you may make it look easy. What those around you don't see is the tremendous amount of hard work and struggle that goes into making things look easy. While you may thrive on the attention and positive response you get from your good work, you need to be careful that you don't box yourself into a situation that leaves you wondering how in the world you're going to succeed.

Prognosis

While many of you may look at this as a good problem to have—particularly if you've never had it—those who have will tell you that it's no picnic when you realize you're in over your head. It's something akin to "The higher they climb, the harder—and faster—they fall." If you don't temper the enthusiasm of those who have unreasonable expectations of your performance, you may suddenly find yourself with nowhere to go but down—and out.

Prescription

The best way to avoid becoming the has-been superstar is to make sure you don't start believing your own press. By this I mean that if you've been experiencing extraordinary success because of your hard work it's easy to fuel the myths about your own invulnerability. Maintaining a sense of humility and realism about your achievements will go a long way in moderating other's expectations of you. If you don't allow others to place you on a pedestal, you'll be less likely to fall off. While the climb to the top can be euphoric, each level of success places increased performance expectations on you. Be honest about your own accomplishments, make sure to give others credit for their part, and be sure to show how you've struggled as well as how you've triumphed; then you'll be less likely to create the sort of persona that's difficult to live up to. Finding yourself unable to meet the demands placed on you is a high price to pay for the glory of being seen as a superstar. You're better off being seen as someone who consistently meets goals and targets than someone who effortlessly exceeds them, because if you're not careful the fruits of your success will turn out to be the seeds of your failure.

THE LONELINESS AND LOW STATUS OF THE LONE RANGER

Symptoms

Wondering why your bold, independent efforts are not being appropriately rewarded and feeling a sense of isolation from your co-workers are sure signs that you've fallen prey to the myth of the lone ranger.

Diagnosis

The ideal of the lone ranger is a throwback to earlier times when rugged individualism was considered the surest path to success. The image of the loner, the person who beat out the competition through shrewd and calculated posturing, is one that has long been the model for the organizational star. However, the onset of the downsized, leaner, and meaner organization, along with the realization that combined brainpower is more valuable than any one brain, has spawned a new ideal. Now it is the team player, not the loner, who has the most to offer and is the most valued. Your ability to empower others, not your ability to overpower them, is what will make you a star in the modern organization.

Prognosis

If you can convince those around you that you understand the new ideal, that you are committed to working cooperatively with them, and that you can develop the skills of a team player, there's a good chance that you can adapt and thrive under the new conditions. If you continue to rely on the loner mystique, you may soon find yourself obsolete.

Prescription

The first thing you need to do is to let people know that you are willing and able to be a team player and then show them that you have the skills to operate that way. What follows are some of the ways team players differ from loners:

Loners	Team Players
Keep a lot of secrets	Communicate openly
Compete	Collaborate
Act independently	Create interdependence with others
Promote themselves	Promote their group
Trust no one	Foster trust throughout the team
Shoulder all responsibility	Share responsibility
Never ask for help	Seek help frequently and openly

If you want to remain a loner and risk the isolation and diminished impact that such a stance is likely to have in the modern organization, continue practicing the behaviors in the left column. If you want to reach your full potential and help others in your organization to reach theirs, start and keep practicing the behaviors in the right column.

INCREASED TIME PRESSURE AND WHAT TO DO ABOUT IT

Symptoms

One of the most common complaints in the modern working person's life is "Where did the time go?" People suffering from this ailment often feel as though time "literally flew out of their hands," compared to those without the affliction, who feel that "time is on their side." By many experts' accounts, time is, for many people, the poverty of the 1990s. While economic pressures still weigh heavily on most people, it is time poverty—the lack of time—that is often more frustrating.

Diagnosis

While you can't control time, you can control your responses to it. Time management is complex. Your personal level of productivity, your ability to prevent and manage stress, and your ability to balance all the important aspects of your life influence your ability to master your use of time. Earlier in this chapter I discussed strategies for handling stress. In the next chapter I'll talk about how to balance all the key elements in your life. In addition to taking care of those pivotal concerns, you need to address that key time management tool, your personal productivity.

Prognosis

Mastering time management involves three primary areas. Your success in harnessing the ticking clock will be determined to a great extent by your ability to set clear, attainable, yet challenging goals; set priorities; and eliminate unnecessary tasks. This information is probably not new to you. The problem with these three things is that they're more easily said than done. However, if you can truly gain control over these areas, you're on your way to becoming the master of your time rather than its victim.

Prescription

First let's look at goals. For one thing, goals are illusive. We don't always know what we want. For another, they are changing. It's unlikely that at this moment you have the same goals as you had last year. You've probably reached some of those goals and have moved on. You've probably also—if you're a risk taker—established some goals you haven't yet reached. If you're not careful, you're hanging on to some goals that you should have abandoned months ago. The point is that goal setting is a fluid, ever-changing process that needs to be checked and rechecked on an ongoing basis. You may be thinking that you're too busy to bother doing that. This is dangerous because in essence you're saying, "I'm too busy putting out fires to pay attention to my goals." The problem is that what this really means is that you're too busy doing things that distract you from your goals to do the things that would help you reach your goals. More simply put, you're too busy doing the unimportant things to do the important ones.

This brings us to the next key time management skill, setting priorities. This is a simple, familiar notion, most simply stated as doing "first things first." If you operate systematically by nature, you will have a much easier time with this than if you are someone who prefers to "go with the flow." The problem with "going with the flow" in relation to time management is that you can lose a lot of valuable time if you find yourself down the wrong branch of the river. If you're someone who systematically sets priorities, the important thing to do is to make sure you follow through on completing your predetermined list in priority order. If you're someone who is unlikely to set priorities in any formal way, the important thing is to find a means of setting priorities that is user friendly to you. Develop a technique that is most likely to work for you, and find ways to monitor your progress. Build in rewards for following your strategy, and you'll be more likely to succeed at it.

The third key to effective time management is the elimination of unnecessary tasks. Many of these are probably already familiar to you: an overcluttered desk that gets reshuffled repeatedly, staying on the phone longer than necessary to get what you need, approaching the wrong people for what you need, handling the same piece of paper over and over instead of getting rid of it the first time, and simply procrastinating because you're uncomfortable or anxious about doing what needs to be done. Conducting a critical analysis of those unnecessary tasks you perform on a regular basis can go a long way in helping you manage your time.

Consider this: If you were to set goals effectively, prioritize them, and eliminate unnecessary tasks, you could easily save two hours a day (a modest figure), which would be the equivalent of having 30 extra days a year. Imagine the headway you could make in your career if you had 13 months a year to work, the benefits to your family and marriage if you had an extra month a year to spend with them, or the rest and relaxation you would get from a month's vacation each year.

It sounds so simple—just stop doing those things that waste your time. Then how come so many of us have so much trouble doing it? One reason you may have already suspected is that this is not as simple as it at first seems. Human beings are complex; our minds are not simple. In fact, people do things everyday that boggle the mind. I'd like you to consider that failing to understand the psychology of time managment is one of the biggest obstacles to achieving success in controlling your time. As I explained in the first chapter, one way people can do themselves in is through self-talk. You may remember that one of the characteristics of successful people is that they use positive self-talk. They constantly remind themselves of their ability to succeed at what they attempt, unlike people who frequently use negative self-talk—and who tend to be less successful. Positive self-talk by someone who is good at time management might sound like this: "I am in control of my time. Time is a constant. If I make the right choices, I will have all the time I need. My success is not based on having too much to do, but in doing the right things and in doing things right." Negative self-talk around time management might sound like this: "I'm overloaded. This is too stressful. I'll never get it done. There's just not enough time." This can be debilitating self-talk, but it can get even worse. Remember, this is not simple stuff.

The worst kind of negative self-talk is so strong that it can make you feel totally incapable of managing your time. Negative self-talk can offer a litany of destructive messages: "I'm too lazy, I'm too disorganized, I don't know how to take control, I'm a failure, and I've always been like this." This sort of self-talk will convince you that things are hopeless. If you can transform these messages into positive self-talk, you'll be on your way to making things work. For example, try replacing "I'm too disorganized" with "With a little help, I could get organized—and here's my chance"; "I'm really not a failure at managing my time—I've just never really committed myself to it totally, and maybe this is a good time to start"; or "I'm tired of being the victim, and I'm ready to take the bull by the horns." Simply put, shift your attitude and you've taken the first big step toward getting a handle on managing your time.

Time is one of those few aspects of our lives that moves forward regardless of what we do. Every 60 seconds another minute passes, every 60 minutes another hour passes, and so on. If you think about it, it's easy to see why so many of us feel so out of control and unable to manage this elusive and constant thing called time. Add to that the complexity of the age, and things really get messy. Consider what technology has done to our ability to manage time. The computer, the fax machine, and the cellular phone are technological advances that hypothetically created an opportunity for us to make the most of our time. Many people suggested that this technology would in fact give us more time (a physical impossibility). There is no such thing as more time, only better use of one's time.

Unfortunately, what the technology could have provided, it hasn't, probably because we didn't let it. Our time's biggest enemy is probably ourselves. For instance, anyone who does a fair amount of writing knows what a blessing a word processor is compared to a typewriter; it's kind of like the difference between writing on walls with stones and the invention of the pencil. Or consider the difference between fax and U.S. Mail or between U.S. Mail and the Pony Express. When was the last time you waited for an important document to arrive in the mail? You don't because you don't have the time. You also know that the person who needs something from you today is not going to wait two days to get it; just as they will not accept a draft of a proposal covered with scratched-out pencil marks. They want it fast and perfect. So much for time being on your side. Instead of technology saving you time, it has done just the opposite—made the demands on your time and people's expectations of you more intense. It's as though someone grabbed the control knob of the treadmill, speeded it up, and requred you to run the rat race all that much faster. What I'm suggesting is that you owe it to yourself, to your career, and to your organization to regain control by grabbing the reins, setting your pace, and ensuring that you arrive at your chosen destination on time, every time. Here's how.

Thirty Things You Can Do to Save Time Today

1. **Organize Your Time Realistically.**   Poor organization is the biggest threat to your time management. There are all kinds of planners, calendars, and time management systems available. The important thing is to get yourself organized in a way that works for you and *use it*.
2. **Catch Yourself Wasting Time and Stop.**   The key to getting rid of the time wasters is to catch yourself early on before you've gotten too involved and find yourself beyond the point of no return.
3. **Set Clear Limits and Obey Them.**   Without boundaries there is chaos. Don't allow yourself to get swept away by the demands around you. Know what your limits are, and keep to them as best you can.

4. **Get Other People to Do Things for You.** Think about the best time managers you know, people who really get things done. Chances are good that they are expert delegators. They delegate down, up, and across the organization.

5. **Streamline Routine but Necessary Tasks.** We all have things to do that are tedious and eat up our time. Some of these things are unavoidable. Find ways to do them that are as quick and as pleasant as possible.

6. **Create Multiple Agendas.** Whenever you can, do things that satisfy more than one person or meet more than one need. For example, produce the kind of report that impresses both your boss and your customers or clients.

7. **Never Wait.** A key time-saving strategy, this area is so important that it will be covered in depth later in this section.

8. **Take Short Breaks When You Need Them.** No one has unlimited energy, yet it is amazing what a brief respite can do for you. Find ways to give your mind and body a rest after peak busy periods, and you'll be amazed how it helps you to keep going.

9. **Use Your Mind during Physical Activity.** During physical activity, the mind is often at its most stimulated and potentially creative, yet few people take full advantage of this opportunity to come up with new ideas or solve problems.

10. **Catch Yourself Using Negative Self-Talk and Get Rid of It.** As mentioned earlier, this is a killer. One technique that can work is to practice transforming negative messages into positive ones. If you can do this, your attitude and productivity will improve dramatically.

11. **Don't Worry about Time-Consuming Things that You Have No Control Over.** While taking control is a key to effective time management, there are things over which you have no control. Don't fight them. Just do them.

12. **Listen Actively the First Time You Hear Something Important.** Probably the most overlooked tool for time management is good listening. Imagine how much time you

would save if every time you heard something important you heard it right the first time. Imagine how much less frustrated you would be and how much less time you would spend worrying about the wrong things.

13. **Keep Your Personal Work Space Organized.** People waste phenomenal amounts of time looking for things in a disorganized space. Techniques like keeping only one pile of paper work wonders. Try this tip: If you're a clutter rat, start throwing out a full trash can of stuff a day until the clutter is gone. You'll be amazed at how long it takes you to run out of worthless stuff.

14. **Get Off the Phone.** This is another important point that will be covered in depth later. Just consider for a moment the time saved if you limited yourself to saying—and hearing—things that mattered and eliminated the superficial or insignificant parts of the conversation.

15. **Handle Every Important Item on Your Agenda Immediately, or as Soon as Possible.** This is the old priority push being hammered home again; it's that important.

16. **Prioritize the Do's and Move through Them Methodically.** Even the most "shoot from the hip" personalities will feel a sense of relief once they've figured out which of the important things they'll do first.

17. **Concentrate on One Thing at a Time.** One surefire way of shooting your well-intentioned self in the foot is to split your attention between two important things simultaneously and end up giving neither of them the attention they need.

18. **If You Find Yourself Resisting a Task, Find Another One to Do First.** Why fight your own resistance? As long as there's another important task waiting in the wings (there usually is), why not move on? When you come back to the tough one after a success, you're apt to be reenergized and ready to tackle it.

19. **When You've Done Something Well, Leave It Alone.** This reflects the familiar "If it ain't broke. . . ." The problem is that many people dwell on tasks longer than they need to in the name of perfection. While perfection may

be an admirable trait to some, it can be the kiss of death for effective time management.

20. **Disregard Unimportant Agendas.** Make sure everything you do is worth doing. If you're not sure, why not do something you're sure is important first?

21. **Build in Periodic Progress Checks Every Day.** The best way to know how you're doing is to check on it. That way you're not at the end of the day and out of time before you realize you need to shift gears.

22. **Catch Other People Wasting Your Time and Stop Them.** Identify the distractors in your life and learn ways to cut them off at the pass. Otherwise, they'll kill your time every chance they get.

23. **Say No to Other People's Demands Unless You Can Think of a Good Reason to Say Yes.** One of the best ways to protect your time is to say no. The more successful you are, the more demanding other people will be of your time. While it's important to say yes to the important requests, being selective can be a real time saver.

24. **Schedule Your Time with Other People into the Shortest Blocks of Time Possible.** This is where the old maxim "The amount of work expands to fit the time available" comes into play. This strategy works even with people who steal your time. Think about it. Give a person an hour; they take an hour and 15 minutes. Give people half an hour; they take 45 minutes. Your saving is 30 minutes.

25. **Limit Your Social Interaction to Important Relationships.** While it's important to have good, friendly relations with people at work, being open to idle conversation can eat up any discretionary time you have. Choose your conversations carefully and develop graceful ways to exit insignificant conversations and you'll be far better off than if you're considered an open ear to everyone.

26. **Eliminate Small Talk from Your Conversations with Everyone.** Nobody really wants to talk about the weather, so why do we always do it? Cut to the chase and get to the heart of the matter, and others will learn to be more direct with you as well. It'll save you all a lot of time.

27. **When You Need a Problem Resolved, Go to the Person Who Has the Power to Solve It.**   Much time is wasted on going through channels. While it's sometimes important from a political perspective to go through the proper channels, there are many times that it makes more sense to bypass the gatekeepers and go right to the source. Know who the person is who has the power to solve your problem and whenever possible deal with that person directly.

28. **Use Your Travel Time.**   People often complain about the way travel "eats up time." Technology has eliminated that problem. Whether you're flying, driving, or sitting on the train, you can use portable computers, cellular phones, and portable tape recorders to help you generate ideas, plan activities, or respond to clients or customers. There's no reason to treat this valuable time as a loss.

29. **Establish a Quitting Time at the Beginning of the Day and Stick to It.**   This idea is getting increased press and increased support lately. The reality is that most people's level of productivity diminishes dramatically after eight or nine hours of work, so why fight it?

30. **Make the Most of Every Moment.**   This last bit of advice is perhaps the most important. As I mentioned earlier, time is constant; what varies is the effectiveness of our use of it. Adopt this piece of advice as your motto, and you've won half the battle. Remember, time is one of your richest resources; when you make the most of it, you enhance your performance and enrich your life.

While endless things can sap your time, research on time indicates that there are four areas that consume the most time for most people: the telephone, meetings, your boss, and waiting. I've already touched on each of them briefly in this section. Here are some practical tips on how to handle each of these time drains.

Twelve Tips for Managing the Telephone   An unquestionably invaluable tool, the telephone can become an albatross. Cellular phones in golf carts and portable faxing from the beach are just two examples of how the phone, if you're not careful, can become your ball and chain. Here's how to make the most of this valuable but potentially imposing tool.

1. **Develop a Plan for Screening, Delegating, and Consolidating Phone Calls.** This idea is especially for you if you find yourself with the phone growing out of your ear. If you simply respond to or can't resist that little box, you will become its slave. You need a strategy that protects you from the monopoly phone calls can have on your time.

2. **State What You Want as Early in the Conversation as Possible.** Get past the amenities and state your need quickly and clearly.

3. **Make Sure Those You're Talking with Are Ready to Talk with You.** Aside from showing consideration for other people's time, this tactic will also save you time and energy. If you've caught someone at a bad time, chances are slim that you'll get what you need. You're better off reconnecting with them when they're ready to give their full attention.

4. **Avoid Distracting Conversation on the Phone; Get and Keep to the Point of the Call.** In a funny way, the telephone invites distraction. Part of the problem is that phone contact lacks the immediacy of face-to-face contact. There's no body language or subtle nonverbal cues to rely on. Because of this, people can easily drift from the point of the conversation in an effort to establish rapport. The problem is that the conversation can go far afield and cost you valuable time. One way to avoid this is to prepare for your calls ahead of time; sit upright, focus on your purpose for calling, and state clearly what you want from the onset of the conversation. Repeat it as clearly as possible as often as necessary. Your conversations will be crisper and more fruitful.

5. **Repeat What You Want in as Many Ways as You Can Until It Gets Responded to.** Take a tip from fund-raisers who make it a point to ask for money at least three times in a conversation, in as many different ways as they can think of.

6. **Monitor the Length of Phone Contact. Keep and Set Limits on Conversation Time.** When all else fails, the best time management tool is a clock. Set reasonable limits for the length of conversations according to the business at hand, and stick to those limits.

7. **Be Relentless in Your Pursuit of Disconnection. Have and Use Reasons to Get Off the Line.** Some people like to chat after completing the business of a call. As soon as you've taken care of business, let the other person know you're ready to get off. If you've got somewhere to be or another call to take, all the better. If you can, avoid rudeness, but don't be afraid to be direct about your desire to say goodbye.

8. **Keep a Record of Problem Callers and Develop Strategies for Handling Them.** For people who continually steal your time via the telephone, the best defense is a good offense. When they say, "Have you got a minute?" say, "That's about all I have. What can I do for you?" If they don't tell you, keep asking them that same question until you get a direct answer. Then give them what they want or tell them that you're sorry you can't and get off.

9. **Avoid Making Social Calls.** This is for those of you who use the phone to distract yourselves from distasteful tasks. While the ease of picking up the phone for a friendly chat—and even convincing yourself that you're doing it in the name of networking—is tempting, it can really put a dent in your productivity. If you must make social calls, limit your conversations to five minutes.

10. **Make Use of All Available Technology, including Call Waiting, Voice Mail, Conference Calling.** One way to screen calls if you don't have a person to do it for you is with the use of at least an answering machine and at best an answering service or voice mail system that can field calls when you can't or don't have the time to take them. A good strategy that is way underutilized when you're working with several people on a project is the conference call. It can save you a great deal of time and duplication of effort.

11. **Establish and Maintain Quiet Hours When You Receive No Calls.** While this may not be an option for some of you, it is possible for many people who do not use it. Setting aside one or two hours a day when you allow yourself freedom from distracting phone calls can be a real boon to your productivity.

12. **When the Need to be Uninterrupted Is Acute, Leave Your Phone's Area of Reach.** There are times when the best thing to do is leave your office and tell no one where you can be reached. Most people can't do this too often for too long, but it's amazing how much you can accomplish in an hour or less of totally uninterrupted time. Give yourself the option when you really need it.

Ten Steps to More Productive Meetings The figures vary, but research suggests that most people whose work includes meetings spend 50 percent to 80 percent of their time in those meetings. The current emphasis in many organizations on teamwork will most likely mean even more meeting time. While there is no surefire way to make every meeting a productive one, there are things you can do—whether you are in charge of the meeting or just a participant—that can contribute to their effectiveness. Here are ten ideas that can help a great deal.

1. **Make Sure the Purpose of the Meeting Is Clear to You and Other Attendees.** "Why are we here?" is the question. "Because this is the scheduled time for our meeting" is not a good answer if you're serious about improving productivity.

2. **Make Sure Everyone Is Aware of the Agenda for the Meeting.** This should be done in writing prior to the meeting so that everyone has a copy going in or at least at the beginning of the meeting.

3. **Pose Questions to be Considered Prior to the Meeting.** If you can get people focused on the problems you're trying to solve before the start of the meeting, there's all the more chance that the session itself will offer well-thought-out ideas rather than knee-jerk reactions.

4. **Ask Others to Gather and Bring Pertinent Information to the Meeting.**   Along the same lines as point 3, if there is external information—valuable data that can help you in the meeting—better to have it there the first time than to have to schedule another meeting once the information is gathered.

5. **Make Sure the Right People Are at the Meeting.**   Meeting behavior can become habitual, and you can find the make-up of the group driving the meeting instead of the agenda. Generally, the smaller the group, the less complex, so keep the group small and save the nonessential players for times when you really need them.

6. **Start the Meeting on Time and End It on Time.**   This is the simplest yet most powerful time-saving strategy you can use. Develop a reputation for starting late and watch how people adapt by always being late. End on time and you keep everyone's attention; otherwise, they begin fretting about where they need to be next and you lose them, if not in body then in mind, which is what counts.

7. **Don't Allow Outside Interruptions.**   Enforcing this might be tough, but it's a good idea to establish a norm that keeps outside distractions at a minimum. You don't have to be hard-nosed about this; simply suggest that more will be accomplished without interruptions, and ask everyone involved to keep them to a minimum.

8. **Keep to the Agenda.**   If the discussion shifts, be sure to return to the agenda items at hand. It's inevitable that even the most smoothly run meeting gets off track. Sometimes the digression is worthwhile; sometimes it isn't. Regardless, it's important to remember that the priority for this meeting is to get done what you set out to do. It will set the standard for other meetings and for people's expectations in the future.

9. **Summarize Conclusions to Each Agenda Item before Moving On.**   Even the most attentive attendees will drift off the focus on occasion. To bring them back in line and to ensure that everyone agrees on what has transpired, summarize group decisions and plans periodically.

10. **Decide the Next Steps before Adjourning.** To avoid stalled progress, determine the next steps before you let people go, figure out what you need from them, and make sure they know before leaving the meeting what they have to do. This will save you invaluable time and avoid unnecessary follow-up.

These ten suggestions represent simple steps you can take to make your meetings more efficient and effective. Implementing and encouraging this sort of tightly run meeting behavior can make a dramatic difference whether you're in charge or in a support role.

Seven Ways to Avoid Your Boss's Drain on Your Time

Your relationship with your boss is one of the key variables influencing your success at work. While you sometimes have to give your boss more of your time than you would like, there are ways of managing the relationship that will protect your time. Here are some tips for managing your boss's drain on your time.

1. **Determine What Your Boss Has to Offer You that Will Help You Do Your Job.** No boss is perfect—each has strengths and liabilities. Unless your boss is a real monster (in which case no amount of time management will help), your best bet is to focus on her or his strengths and ignore the weaknesses. Figure out what your boss can help you with and ask for help at strategic points in time.

2. **Ask for What You Want in a Way that Is Likely to Get a Positive Response.** If you can figure out what matters to your boss, you can present your requests in a way that is likely to elicit a positive response. This will ensure that you spend less time having to persuade your boss—or worse, having to change his or her mind. Know what works with the boss and what doesn't; then use strategies that are likely to succeed.

3. **Determine What Your Boss Wants from You.** Figure out what the expectations and the key success factors are for your performance, and that's half the battle. If you know what is wanted, you don't have to waste a lot of time second-guessing, which wastes your boss's time and yours.

4. **Give Your Boss What He or She Wants.** You will lose an enormous amount of time resisting your boss's wishes. Make it a habit to provide what your boss wants, even if you don't think it's needed, and you'll save a lot of time. You might even save your job. People who think their work is all that matters to make their jobs secure miss the point that in these volatile times, you also need to have a strong relationship with your boss.

5. **Learn Your Boss's Patterns and Make Your Approach When He or She Is Most Receptive.** Here, timing is everything. Catching your boss fresh and rested rather than tired and stressed can make a big difference in the response you get. Get to know your boss's patterns—good times and bad times—and ask about the important things when your boss is likely to be up.

6. **Let Your Boss Know What You're Doing as Often as Possible.** This is just a safety measure. It's quick and easy to keep a boss informed. It's a lot better than having to spend a lot of time backpedaling because you failed to let her or him know what you were up to.

7. **Treat Your Boss Like a Valued Client or Customer.** Like our relationships with our relatives, relationships with our bosses can become comfortable to the point where we take them for granted. To avoid problems, treat your boss with sensitivity and care. Do not assume anything, and you'll be less likely to regret anything.

These simple tips, most of them common sense, will increase the likelihood that your boss feels involved, informed, and in control of your work—and will consequently stay out of your hair.

Ten Ways to Get Rid of the Waits   Waiting around for other people who are not doing a very good job of managing their time—or who are just plain too busy—can prove to be a real time waster unless you're prepared for it, in which case it can be a real opportunity. Here's how to turn a potential annoyance into a potential opportunity.

1. **Avoid Waiting by Confirming Appointments Right before You Leave for Them.** This is a quick and easy way to

avoid appointment gridlock and to let someone know that you expect them to be ready for you shortly.

2. **Always Have a Problem in Your Head that Requires Creative Thinking to Solve.**   The best way to eliminate waiting time is to be prepared for it. If you find yourself in a waiting situation that is conducive to thinking (a long and quiet one), having a key project and maybe some notes on it to work on can prove to be a very fruitful use of your waiting time.

3. **Brainstorm Potential Solutions to Nagging Problems.** Brainstorming, the process of generating an uncensored list of possible alternatives, is a valuable practice that many of us use less frequently than we could because time constraints often get in our way. A good way to use waiting time is to pick a problem that's been nagging you and make a no-holds-barred list of possible solutions. If you come up with a useful one in the process (as often happens), you'll have turned a potentially wasted period into a timesaving period.

4. **Always Have Something to Read With You.**   In this information age, none of us has all the time we need to keep up with advances in our field or with current events. Making sure you've got some worthwhile reading material with you when you are facing a potential waiting situation makes good use of what might have been wasted time.

5. **Keep a Personal Planner or Time Management Organizer with You At All Times.**   Sometimes waiting situations are too noisy or chaotic for any real thinking. The best thing to do in these situations is to catch up on your clerical chores—things that support your work. By using even the shortest block of waiting time to update your personal information file or work notes, you'll be using every minute and making valuable headway.

6. **Plan the Careful Use of Discretionary Days.**   Short blocks of waiting time are also good times to take a look at your schedule. Pay attention to days that are not yet full of activity (if you can't find any, you're in big trouble). Focus

on these days and think about things you could do that you've been wanting to do but haven't had the time for. Use your waiting time to plan these open days carefully to make the most of them. This can be important because the tendency is to whittle these days away when they arrive. Strategic planning can avoid that.

7. **Write Thank You or Catch-Up Notes.** In this fast-paced, time-impoverished age, few people take the time to write thank you notes or to keep in touch with various contacts the way they should. Using waiting time to do this is a great use of otherwise wasted time. Just keep a little stationery, a few envelopes, and some stamps with you. Make sure you keep your address file up-to-date too (not just phone numbers). You'll be amazed how much people will appreciate this small gesture.

8. **Let Those You're Waiting for Know of Your Time Constraints.** People who keep you waiting often assume you're willing to wait indefinitely. Letting others know what your limits are is a way to blow those assumptions out of the water.

9. **Consider Other People's Poor Time Management Inevitable.** This is a good strategy for rage management as well. Many people are poor time managers, and if you expect otherwise you're opening yourself up to disappointment. Stress experts tell us that developing a tolerance for waiting is an important stress management technique. At any rate, it's inevitable, so why fight it?

10. **Consider Waiting Time a Gift of Time.** This is a matter of attitude. If you can transform waiting from being a potential problem into an opportunity, you're on your way to making the most of all your time—even that part of your time that's controlled by other people.

Follow the simple guidelines covered in the preceding section on time management, and you'll find yourself winning the war against time poverty. You may even find yourself with time on your hands. If you do, be sure to do the one thing that most people forget to do with their time when there's not enough of it—enjoy it.

WHAT TO DO WHEN YOU'VE LOST THE COMPANY MONEY

Symptoms

An abundance of redness, particulary in your accounting sheets. Seriously, few things are more threatening to your career than losing money for the organization. However, there are many cases in which the outcome of such a scenario is less than disasterous. Once the symptoms appear, it's important to take action. Damage control early on can avert the emergence of more complicated problems later.

Diagnosis

The first concern is how much. I hope you haven't risked large sums of the company's money foolishly. If you have, perhaps you can take comfort in the corporate lore about the vice president who walks into the president's office to resign after costing the company a million dollars. The president responds by refusing to accept the resignation: "Are you crazy? I just spent a million dollars educating you, and I'm not about to let you leave now."

In all likelihood, you will not have such an understanding boss. Probably you don't have such an overwhelming problem either. However, there are many ways you could find yourself in the dilemma of costing your organization money. You could have made a bad investment, made a poor judgment call, or had a product line fizzle. In any event, it is important that you measure your value to the company as objectively as possible before assuming that your mistake will cost you your job. Then you need to get clear on what happened and why so that you can effectively plead your case.

Prognosis

Chances are if you're a valued employee, one financial mistake won't cost you your job. Everyone makes mistakes, and good people are hard to find. The most important thing you need to do is to be absolutely certain that you understand your company's attitude about mistakes. Are they extremely conservative and do they frown on mistakes, or do they pride themselves on being risk takers? This assessment will help determine which response to the problem will be most effective. A conservative company will expect a cautious, conciliatory response; an innovative company will expect a dynamic, creative one.

Prescription

If your mistake occurred in the context of a more conservative organization, the first thing you need to do is reassure your superiors that it was a one-time event and will not happen again. If you're really nervous, you can present them with a plan for ensuring that such an occurrence will not be repeated. If the rest of your work is consistently good, chances are you will not be penalized for your mistake and will eventually be forgiven.

If your mistake occurred in an organization that encourages risk taking, your response becomes a little more complex. If part of your job involves coming up with innovative approaches to the company's business, you want to be careful that the mistake doesn't cause you to become overcautious. Then again, you don't want to risk having your superiors thinking you're careless or trigger-happy. As long as your risk is perceived as one worth taking by those in charge, you have little to fear in terms of repercussions. Most likely your superiors will be looking to see if you're someone who can bounce back from defeat, regain your composure, and come up with new risks that are likely to succeed.

KNOWING WHEN TO QUIT

Symptoms

Finding yourself in a situation where your performance, satisfaction, motivation, or effectiveness is diminishing substantially is a signal that it may be time for you to terminate your employment voluntarily. While it's a good idea to explore all other alternatives before throwing in the towel, far too often people stay longer than they should and find themselves out of a job—or worse, in a job they absolutely cannot tolerate.

Diagnosis

It's important to distinguish truly justifiable reasons to quit from all the other scenarios that might push you to the brink. Most important is to discern whether your motivation to quit is the result of an acute or chronic problem. Acute problems can seem overwhelming in their immediacy, yet often diminish in intensity if you can hang in and let the problem run its course. Undesirable or demanding assignments; problem subordinates, superiors, or colleagues; or changing organizational conditions may lead you to the point of quitting. The question you should be asking yourself is: "Is the source of my dissatisfaction temporary or is it chronic?" If it's temporary, do what you need to do to outlast it. If it's chronic, you'd better start thinking seriously about whether it's time for you to move on.

Prognosis

While deciding you have to quit can feel like the worst thing possible, it's important to remember that it's not the end of the world. In fact, deciding that a job and an organization are no longer for you before the organization decides you're no longer for them gives you an advantage. As soon as you decide it's time to move on, you can begin planning and implementing your search. If you wait to be terminated, you'll experience greater time pressure, plus you'll have the disadvantage of having been let go—becoming the victim instead of the decision maker. Even during difficult times, jobs open up constantly. People retire, die, relocate, or, like you, decide to quit—thus leaving openings available for you to fill. While it's true that it's tougher to find a job during economic down-swings, those who search effectively will find the ones that are available.

Prescription

Conventional wisdom says that it's easier to find a job when you have a job. This leads to the assumption that if at all possible you should never quit a job until you have another one lined up. Like most conventional wisdom, this holds some truth; also like most conventional wisdom, however, there are unconventional conditions that challenge the basic assumption. In this case the challenge has to do with tolerance. There may be times when your current job is driving you so crazy that unless you get out of it you'll be unable to perform at all. If you find yourself in this kind of situation, you need to be careful that you don't get so unmotivated, demoralized, and discouraged that not only do you do a bad job at work, but you do a bad job of looking for new work as well. If you stay too long in a job, you run the risk of creating ill will among people you work with, and it becomes a vicious cycle. You hate the work, stop performing, and create a hostile response in those around you. Your hatred for your work demoralizes you, your poor performance causes you to doubt your competence, and your ability to persuade future employers of your worth and your alienation from others lead to a lack of support for your search and poor references.

While most people dread telling their employer they're planning on leaving because they fear repercussions, in reality most employers, once they recover from the initial shock, will do what they can to help you move on. Some do this because they appreciate your honesty with them and respect your decision, others because they're anxious to see you move on so they can replace you with a more suitable person.

Regardless of the response you get, what's important here is that you do not overextend your stay in a position that is no longer a good match. Whether you choose to find new work before quitting or quit before finding new work, remember that knowing when to quit will save you and those around you unneccesary grief from a prolonged mismatch.

In all of this talk about the impact of your job on your career, it's important to remember that you and only you are responsible for your own success, your own productivity, and your own happiness. Finding others who support you in these efforts is wonderful and can certainly be a boost to your career, but in this turbulent world of work it is crucial to keep in mind that you and you alone have the power and responsibility to create the career you want. Remember, there are three things you can do with your job: enjoy it, change it, or leave it. Nothing else makes much sense.

SIX

Achieving Balance — Doctor's Orders

THE FIVE ELEMENTS OF A BALANCED LIFE

Perhaps the greatest challenge facing each of us in our quest for career wellness is finding a way to balance the various aspects of our lives. We live in a time when the world is out of balance. We see this in the threat to the natural ecosystem, in the distribution of wealth, in the distribution of global power, and in the way many of the people around us live their lives. If you consider for a moment that in the balanced life a person spends an equal amount of time and energy focused on each of five areas—work, family and friends, play and recreation, learning, and social responsibility—most people would be hard-pressed to think of anyone they know who lives a balanced life.

In reality, I believe there are people who lead balanced lives; however, their balance is not quite as neat. Few, if any, live a life in which they equally commit 20 percent of their time and energy to each of the five key areas. I don't even know if that's an ideal to aspire to. What I do know is that people who ignore any of the five key elements to a balanced life are living a life out of balance—one sure to catch up with them eventually.

When I first started writing about this, I looked for people who had moved from a life out of balance to one that was more balanced; what I found confirmed that each person's version of balance is unique. In fact, the more I interviewed people the more I came to realize that not only was each one's version of balance unique, but that each one's understanding of the nature of balance—and it's relevance to career wellness— was also unique. What excited me most about my quest for understanding balance was that each person seemed to have his or her own way of making sense of the world and the work in a way that worked for the individual. Some of the people discussed in this chapter had critical events occur in their lives that caused them to focus more on balance; for others, achieving balance has been a lifelong endeavor. I hope their stories help you get closer to achieving your own center of balance.

CHANGES OF THE HEART

The people I'm going to talk about now are unique in that their life experience created a dramatic sequence of events leading to a shift from a life out of balance to a life of balance. Although their experiences are unique, I believe the lessons they have to offer are universal.

Bill T.—Creating Change through Action

I first met Bill T. when he asked me to work with him, helping a local Chamber of Commerce develop a strategic plan. I was immediately struck with his social consciousness and his commitment to making his town a better place for all to work and live. The more time I spent with Bill, the more impressed I was with the extent to which he seemed to live a balanced life. He seemed to enjoy his work, had a good relationship with his wife, was always challenging my thinking by presenting other points of view—and he could tell me where the best restaurants were in any city he had been to in the last three years. In short, it seemed that his work, family, social responsibility, learning, and leisure sides were all flourishing in full swing.

As I got to know Bill, I came to find that his life was not always this balanced. In fact, had I met Bill six years before, I would have met quite a different man. At that time Bill was a materials manager for a major computer company. His job often demanded that he spend 60 to 70 hours a week working. "I wasn't a workaholic," says Bill, "but when you have a job that requires that you work 60 to 70 hours a week, you do it." Until you have a heart attack! In April of 1985, Bill suffered a major heart attack while playing racquetball. "There wasn't much pain. It was as if someone flipped a switch and all my systems shut down."

Before Bill's heart attack forced him to look at creating changes in his life, he was clearly on a fast paced career track. Once he got his first job in materials management, he began to move up the organizational ladder. "There's a belief on some people's parts that the higher you go, the less work you do. That's not true in manufacturing management. It tends to get more hectic the higher you go, and the pressure tends to build rather than decrease. It's a tremendously demanding business without a lot of break time. It's not the kind of thing you can do for very long if you don't like it because it's a kind of punishing environment. But if you like it, as I did, the stress levels get higher, the responsibilities get greater, the number of people reporting to you grows, the impact you have on the plant—good and bad—gets greater, which adds more stress."

Just prior to his heart attack, Bill was his plant's chief materials manager with close to 300 people reporting to him, working on a new product line in an extremely stressful environment. "The pressure was tangible; you could see it in people's faces and feel it in the building. Personally, while I was 50, I was in good shape, my weight was down, I was playing racquetball three times a week, I didn't feel imbalanced, but I was going at full speed."

Like many men who have stress-related heart trouble, Bill had no outward signs that he was close to having a heart attack. After the heart attack, Bill got into a cardiac rehab program, which he says was probably the start of his change in life-style. Shortly after returning to work (five months later), it became clear to Bill that he could no longer keep doing his job—and live very long. "Initially I believed that I could still do my job with some changes. That worked for a few months until the product development cycle began again; I realized I couldn't control the stress, and I started to show physical symptoms. The message was clear, 'you can't do that job anymore.' "

He began discussions with the plant manager; although there were no immediate options available, the two of them agreed to "keep their eyes open." Over the next several months there was a plant offsite meeting, a strategic plan developed for the plant, and the possibility of several position changes. Most of the possibilities didn't appeal to Bill. "I'd always been a real hands-on guy, and the thought of moving into a staff position that would be less stressful, but also less challenging, really didn't appeal to me. I've always been interested in doing things that are concrete as opposed to abstract, to be able to influence improvements, and to get things done—those have always been my prime drivers."

It wasn't until Bill saw the write-up for a new position that was being created by the plant manager—who was soon to leave the plant—that Bill got excited. The position was for a manager of community and area relations. "This was the first position to come along that had the hands-on feel of a line position without some of the intense pressure of my old job, and I decided to go for it." What he saw was not simply a public relations position, but a position focused on creating a positive impact in the community. "This was the first position to come along that got me really excited. It just clicked. It fit everything I like to do without the stresses of operational responsibility. It was a little scary, but I saw it as an opportunity to grow in a totally new situation and environment. One of the driving forces for me was the social responsibility piece. I believed that I could help and make a positive contribution. Once I realized the organization wanted to support real community involvement (not just giveaways), I felt that there was a lot I could do that could have a lasting impact on the community."

When I asked Bill about other changes that coincided with this change in work role, he offered several responses. "One of the other changes is that I started spending more time at home with my family. If you're spending all that time at work, you're obviously not home much. My social life has improved, too. It used to be that when my wife asked me if I wanted to go to the movies and I'd been working all day on Saturday, my response would be, Do I have to? I go to more dinner parties, too."

One of the important aspects of the change expressed by Bill is that he gave up what was wrong with his past job without giving up what was right with it. "I feel just as challenged as I did in the operational job. I'm breaking new ground, dealing with new problems, seeing new issues. Just like the challenges in developing a new product, there's no blueprint that tells you how to fix it; you have to figure it out yourself. I don't have any less job satisfaction today—and that's a surprise. If someone told me I would be happy in a nonoperational job I wouldn't have believed them. In retrospect, I would never go back to my old job and do it the way I did it, even if my heart were miraculously back to the way it was before. I would carry less of the load and depend more on the group, but even then I might hesitate. I'm happy with things the way they are now."

Don D.—Portrait of a Scientist

I met with Don D. for this interview in his home on a Sunday afternoon. He and his wife were packing for a trip. He was going to India on business and his wife was going with him. They would spend a week vacationing in India prior to Don's reporting for work. His wife would come home, and Don would continue on to Europe to conduct additional business. The trip is a good illustration of Don's ability to integrate work, family, leisure, learning, and social responsibility.

Don D. is a Senior Fellow and manager at Monsanto Corporation. He considers himself above all a scientist. In 1987 he suffered a heart attack. While he does not necessarily feel his heart attack was responsible for major changes in his life, he does believe his sense of balance has changed over the years. He believes that stress was the source of his problems, since he did not suffer from any of the other cardiac risk factors. One way his life changed was that right after the heart attack, he did not have the physical capacity to work the way he used to, although eventually he got it back. The most important thing for him at work is having control of his situation and having the confidence and commitment of those around him. "I don't think of myself as career oriented, but rather as work oriented; that's where being a scientist fits in. If I wanted to be president of the company, I'd have to focus on a lot of things that don't interest me. I'm fortunate in that I have found work that involves doing things I love. It's the ongoing scientific inquiry that gives me my drive. I don't mind working a lot because I'm genuinely interested in what I do."

When I asked him about the role learning plays in his life, he said, "I'm always learning new things; as a scientist you have to if you want to stay on top of new developments and changes in your field. When you're a scientist, learning is built in; it's part of what you're doing, whatever you're doing." When I asked him about relationships at work and how he saw his role he said, "When it comes to relationships at work, I'm always looking to develop people so we're not just putting round pegs in round holes but finding ways to make the most of everyone and meet their needs at the same time. I'm fortunate in that I've built a base in my career and have security in that I know those above me want to know what I think, respect my opinions, and are willing to hear me out. As a result I'm able to offer other people the same opportunity."

Next I asked Don about family life and creating balance in his relationships at home. "In terms of family, the balance shifts. You spend more time with your kids when you're young. When they're gone, you have to find ways to be with each other that are not focused on the kid. I'm lucky in that my wife and I like art and traveling, so we can share that."

The biggest change that Don sees from his heart attack has to do with life-style. "Every day I take a three-mile walk through the neighborhood, which gives me my daily exercise. I've changed my eating habits so that I eat more healthily—no more eggs or red meat." Get him to talk about his photography, and he really lights up. "The thing that hooked me on photography was the electronics and the gadgetry, getting the right light and settings and all that's involved with taking a great picture." Even in leisure that core of being a scientist comes through. He found ways to relax and still tap his core—his love of science.

Another change Don says he experienced after his heart attack was being more of a risk taker. "I started to appreciate things more and take more careful chances. I'm also very interested in world events. I often read the magazines and newspapers cover to cover. More important, though, through traveling I have met people face to face in their countries often during times of crisis. This enables you to cut through the politics and see things the way they really are." When I asked him about his personal sense of social responsibility, Don had this to say: "As a scientist social responsibility kicks in because you're deeply concerned with telling the truth. If an engineer builds a bridge and fudges on the specifications, the bridge can collapse. I'm very much aware of the importance of using science to tell the truth."

One of the ways Don manages his stress is through his sense of humor. "I believe you must maintain and use your sense of humor. I remember a friend called just after I got home from the hospital to see if he could come over and visit me. I could hear the nervousness in his voice and I said, 'I'll try to fit you in between heart attacks.' I could hear his nervousness disappear through the laughter." As I listened to Don, I remembered going to visit him in the hospital just after his heart attack—and I remember what we did was exchange jokes.

Before I left, Don invited me upstairs to see some of his photographs. On the walls were beautiful pictures of Japan, Europe, and various American landmarks. As I left I was struck with how this life of science led to such broad experience, which contributed to one man's balance of work, family, leisure, learning, and social consciousness.

TAPPING AND KEEPING YOUR CAREER CORE

Several things are significant about the profiles of Bill and Don. They are both like many men in American culture in that their work is primary. However, they also seem to have attained a sense of balance in their lives. For both men, the center of their lives is their work. Each identifies strongly with the organization for which he works and each has high expectations for performance. Each of them would tell you that his heart attack sent him a message that he had to change. For Don the change was primarily in the way he handles the stress of his work; for Bill it actually required a change in the nature of the work itself. Perhaps most significant is that both men clearly have what I call a career core.

A career core is a base from which one's work extends and is, for many men, the center of their sense of balance. For Don his center is that he is a scientist; for Bill it is that he is a hands-on creative problem solver. Both men have used their career core to create a balanced life. For Don, science is the basis for his work, his photography hobby, and his search for the truth in understanding world events. For Bill, his hands-on creative problem solving core now focuses on social problems rather than production problems and forms the basis for his work, learning, and social responsibility.

What strikes me about these two men is that both took their circumstances and transformed them—each in his own way—so that their lives are less threatened by the stress created by an imbalance that their work had created. Each used his career core to find ways to alleviate the problem and improve his quality of life. Perhaps most important in all of this is that both men came too close to losing their chance at a balanced life. Perhaps the rest of us can learn from their example and make changes before our bodies alert us to the dangers of a life out of balance.

SPIRITUALITY AND YOUR CAREER

I'd like to speak for a moment to those of you who find your sense of balance through spiritual guidance—and to those of you who don't. I find some people are surprised when they see I've left spirituality out of the balance equation. I'd like to point out that the omission is intentional but should not be misinterpreted to mean that I don't value the spiritual component. On the contrary, I value it highly. In fact, I have found that those who find a spiritual base for their work seem to have a sense of meaning in their work that the rest of us lack. However, spirituality is a very personal thing that defies categorization. The people I know for whom spirituality is central to their lives will tell you that it encompasses all other aspects of living and forms the foundation for the other elements. If that holds some truth for you, I urge you to continue to use it as the basis for your quest for balance. If, however, you feel the absence of spirituality in your life, you may want to consider taking another look at it. It is difficult in this culture to separate religion and spirituality. However, I believe spirituality encompasses religion, and for some religion is the foundation of their spirituality. For others, however, spirituality has little to do with religion but more to do with making sense of one's world and finding a sense of meaning in life. When looked at this way, spirituality clearly plays a role in one's career, for without work that makes sense to you and provides you with some meaning, the likelihood of your being able to sustain yourself through difficult times in your career is slim.

Katja D.—Achieving Balance through Spiritual Growth

I first met Katja D. when she took my Career Renewal workshop series in the summer of 1983. Katja was a partner in a cooperative trucking business and from my perspective was experiencing extreme distress from her frustration in trying to make her business work the way she wanted it to. It was clear that Katja was committed to working in and creating environments that foster participatory, worker-run organizations. Although working in an environment that had the potential to meet this need, it was also clear that her current situation was no longer workable for her. As I speak with Katja now, she is in a job that presents some of the same pressures as her old one, but six years after her transition she feels far more satisfied with her work. When I asked her, as I did of all the interviewees in this chapter, to comment on the five elements of balance, she smiled and said she could not really speak about each separately because for her the nature of the balance lies in the integration of all five elements.

In speaking with Katja, it is clear that she has a deep understanding of herself. She attributes part of this clarity to having been diagnosed with and successfully overcoming cancer, in her case a cancer for which the doctors ascribed a 20 percent chance of survival. Four years later she describes herself as healthy, "healthier than I've ever been." To bring on this "against the odds" state of well-being, she engaged in all the traditional Western and alternative healing methods she could find, including acupuncture and visualization techniques. She considers her response to her cancer diagnosis as key to her current state of balance, both in and outside her work. "For me the key to success in my work is my handling of the difficulties of a job. Before my cancer diagnosis I saw power as outside myself. I didn't feel that I had any power whatsoever. I didn't even know that I could choose what I think, which was for me very revolutionary thinking and part of the reason why I'm still here."

Of all the elements of balance, the one that stood out for me in my conversation with Katja was her emphasis on learning, not as an independent variable, but as a constant. "I work in and choose stressful jobs. For me, the question is always 'What is my learning?' What I've learned in this job is that in my last job I didn't really know how to manage a group as well as I could have; I'm doing that well now and may find I don't need as much of that in my next job. I also think I have some workaholic tendencies, and the more control I have over my life, the less I feel the need to focus so much of my energy on work. The more I understand the need for boundaries, the more balanced I feel in my work, with my kids, and with myself. There was a time when work kept me away from myself; now it helps me understand myself. For me, balance comes every day by focusing on the present, not on my past experience or fear of the future."

Katja is now manager of student-run businesses at a respected university. She sees part of her career core as being a focus on social justice and equality in the workplace. "One of the reasons I became frustrated in my last job was that we were trying to build something very idealistic without the skills to do it." Katja is now completing a doctoral program in Organization Development and has focused much of her study on work teams. "I now have the skills and experience to work effectively in creating and managing teams, and that's very exciting. I'm able to draw on my graduate study and my previous experience to make things work this time. I don't know what my next step will be, but I am sure it will integrate all I've learned and build on those themes of creating social justice and equality in the workplace."

Earlier in this chapter I talked about the spiritual component as a sixth factor that many people include in their quest for balance. When I told Katja I intentionally did not include it, she responded strongly. "You cannot exclude it. In fact it is the center of it all. For me in my work, I struggle with how to integrate it without turning people off. I don't believe you can influence people without paying attention to the spiritual component. By that I mean their belief systems. You need to understand that to understand them. You need to be compassionate with people if you are going to work effectively with them. When I look at a group's or team's behavior, I look at what is actually going on, and then I look at the spiritual side. What beliefs are in the team that are influencing the team? For me, the spiritual side encompasses all the others and brings everything into focus."

Kathleen M.—Balancing a Full Load

"I'm comforted by work," says Kathleen. "When I'm feeling bothered by something, I find a way to focus my energy by finding some work to do. I remember when there was a hurricane threat. I took my kids down into the basement for safety and of course started cleaning the basement."

Kathleen is the assistant director of a branch of a college that specializes in awarding masters' degrees in management to working adults. I asked her for an interview because she seemed to me to be someone who pays attention to all the elements of balance and seemed to integrate them well. "I think I may be a little more frantic than is healthy, although I must admit my body's been the most healthy since I've accelerated my pace.

"The basis for all my action is my family and my need to support them. I feel very fortunate to have a job that I love that enables me to help people from diverse backgrounds. Many of the students I work with have nontraditional backgrounds and might very well not get an advanced degree if they didn't have a program that responded to their particular needs. Helping working adults who share some of the same pressures I do to get degrees is very rewarding."

There are people who misconstrue the notion of balance, thinking it means you shouldn't work so hard. Kathleen is a good example of a balanced person who defies that notion. "Right now I'm working full time, taking nine graduate credits, spending as much time as possible with my children, mountaineering and winter camping as often as I can, and trying to keep everything going at once. It's a struggle at times, but I enjoy it all. The interesting thing for me is that everything I do serves as a metaphor and as learning for everything else. That's one of the reasons I climb mountains. I learn a great deal about life every time I do it."

Several themes were recurrent in almost everything Kathleen talked about: the notion of stretching oneself beyond self-perceived limits, understanding the process involved with exceeding those limits, and her emerging role as a leader. This is evident in her rock-climbing ventures, her struggles with understanding complex statistics in her graduate study, and her efforts toward helping students who are working to stay afloat in their studies. She's recently moved from "seconding" in rock climbing, where she followed another's lead, to "leading," where she sets the ropes and others follow her. She's studying cognitive psychology to understand why she has trouble with statistics, and her recent promotion from Assistant to the Director, overseeing the academic services office, to Assistant Director of the college branch means she has increased responsibility for the school and its mission.

When I suggested to Kathleen that these elements seemed to represent her career core, she tended to agree, but was somewhat hesitant about the leadership part. "Leadership doesn't feel as natural for me as it seems to for men—and I think that's true for many women. There's a process I have to go through to get comfortable leading. I always wanted to follow first. I always wanted someone to check my knots, to check my math, and to tell me what they expect of me in my work. The more confidence I develop, the more willing I am to lead." When I suggested to Kathleen that it seemed to me that one of the differences for many men and women was that men seem focused on outcomes and women also focus on the process for reaching that outcome, she responded: "Who cares about the outcomes! For me the process is everything. I mean outcomes do matter, but how you get there is most important to me. When I'm working with students who are feeling like they can't make it, what I try to do is be there with them and help them to be honest with themselves. I don't always know where they are headed or where the conversation is going, but I try to help them get to where they need to go, wherever that might be."

Our discussion about her transition from Assistant to the Director to Assistant Director reinforced some of what I had already heard about her emerging comfort with leadership. "It's a very new role for me. When I became Assistant Director, people's expectations of me changed, but I just finished leading a very demanding winter ski trip, and I brought everyone back in one piece, so maybe I'm not such a bad leader after all.

"For me the challenge is in becoming a leader and still keeping my feminine side. I think that in our culture men are trained to lead; I think women have to learn it later on. The challenge is to keep the things that are important to me and still be able to feel like more of a leader. The only way you can really be a leader is if you empower other people, and you don't empower people by doing it all yourself or making it seem so difficult that nobody else wants to attempt it. There's a delicate balance there that I'm trying to reach.

"What I do for recreation is write. I love writing about the other things that I'm doing. That's when I really feel relaxed and like I'm having fun, when I'm writing."

I asked Kathleen if I could see some of her writing and she gave me "Beginners Delight," a reference to the name of a rock-climbing route she completed recently at the Shawangunks, a seven-mile stretch of 300-foot vertical cliffs in New York State. Here is an excerpt from that piece (Kathleen is the character Martha):

Beth called down that she had set the anchors and it was okay for Martha to begin the traverse. This was one of the famous parts of the climb, because the only easy way up was to scramble sideways across the cliffs for a distance of almost 30 feet, across rock that was difficult to set protection in. Martha gritted her teeth and unwrapped herself from around the dwarfed tree. Traverses were about the only dangerous part of an ascent for the second climber, because the rope wasn't securely in a vertical position. That meant that if the climber fell, she *could* swing the length of the traverse, instead of just the two or three feet that a second normally plummeted before she was stopped by the rope held by the leader. This particular traverse was a hefty one, and Martha felt grim. She checked her harness, she checked her rope's knot, then she reached behind her to check the knot that held Sandy's rope to her. Three on a climb meant that she was responsible for getting herself, her rope and Sandy's rope to the next anchor point so that Sandy could then be brought up. Otherwise Sandy would be stranded on the rock with no way up or down. But three on a rope meant that not only did Martha have to support her own body while climbing, she also had to pull up the 10 pounds of Sandy's rope, which was compounded exponentially in weight by the friction of it pulling through all the anchoring devices—a phenomenon known as rope drag. In other words, she thought, in a new wave of irritation, it was goddam heavy!

Perhaps the most significant thing that can be learned from examining Kathleen's balancing act is the extent to which each of the five elements overlaps with the others. The drive to strike a balance and integrate all the elements almost seems to be a natural by-product of her actions. Learning is present in every moment of her life, whether she's working with students, studying for school, moving up to the next level in rock climbing, or trying to connect with her children through their interests. Her sense of social responsibility is addressed through her work in helping nontraditional students succeed. "I see myself as a bridge for people, to help them get from where they are to where they want to be. I always try to present alternatives for people that help them to grow. And I guess that's what I try to do for myself as well."

GETTING TO BALANCE

Over the past ten years I've paid very close attention to this thing called "balance" and have been intrigued by the extent to which people are and are not able to achieve it in their lives. I've tried to gain a better understanding of the factors that contribute to leading a balanced life and would like to share some of my observations. I cannot prove any of this, but I have accumulated a great deal of anecdotal evidence to support my view.

Men seem to have a more difficult time than women in getting to balance. There are many theories as to why this is. Some people think it's cultural: Women are forced to balance work and family because they are expected to be the primary caregiver regardless of economic arrangements. Some people think the difference is inherent in the differences between genders: Men are more results oriented and focus more on outcomes, while women are also process oriented and care about how the outcome is reached.

While these are, of course, sweeping generalizations that by their nature beg to be challenged, I do believe that there are differences between the way men and women approach the question of balance and that women seem to have a better handle on it. What this means for you if you are a man is that you have to work harder at finding balance or, more important, recognizing when you're out of balance. What this means for you if you're a woman is that you have to face the threat that your drive toward career advancement places on your potential for getting and keeping balanced.

Regardless of your sex, it seems quite clear that the 1990s will prove challenging for those who seek to live a balanced life. While there has been increased discussion of the importance and value of balance, many forces are operating in opposition to leading a balanced life. Economic difficulties that have forced most two parent families to hold two jobs, large numbers of single-parent families who have no choice, downsized organizations that expect more work from fewer people, and increased educational demands placed on all workers have created conditions likely to threaten anyone's sense of balance.

All this suggests that to create a sense of balance for yourself you have to have a keen awareness of its importance. You can't just let yourself be balanced because it won't happen. You have to be continually aware of the extent to which your activities are focused on the five elements of balance and the extent to which you are neglecting any of them. The key is to keep your focus on all five all of the time. Find ways, as in the examples of balanced people I presented earlier, to integrate the five elements of a balanced life, and you'll find your personal balancing act far less overwhelming. It might not be easy to do, but the results of a balanced life make it well worth doing.

Roberta M.—Weaving for a Living

My interview with Roberta took place in a hotel lounge in Atlanta at 10:00 at night. We'd just finished working with a large corporate client, conducting training on leadership and team building. After about 45 minutes into the conversation, I said to her, "So you're a weaver." She said, "I've never been called a weaver before." I said, "You're a weaver of ideas, of people, and of resources."

"I guess I am. I've always been the organizer when it comes to dealing with social issues that are important to me. I've never just plugged myself into an intact group. I'm always looking to find ways that I can make connections that strengthen the effort.

"I'm not sure I'm as balanced as I could be in terms of the five areas you describe, although they're all very important to me. My kids don't need as much from me now that they're grown—and I'm really grateful I took the time to be with them when they were younger. I try to be playful as much as possible with my family, like doing things with my husband and trying to exercise as much as possible. Right now I'm really busy with work, but I enjoy what I do and that gives me boundless energy. I shock a lot of people. I'll come home after five days of working and I'll collapse that night, but the next morning I'll be ready to go at 8:30 A.M. and do some fun things, and I'll run until 10:00 Sunday night and start packing to leave again Monday morning."

Roberta is well traveled. When her children were young, she and her husband moved to Bangladesh for two years. She has traveled throughout the world and travels regularly for work. I asked her to talk about her love of travel and what being constantly on the move does for her. "I love seeing and learning about different cultures. If someplace is going to offer me a new perspective, I'm ready to go."

Roberta is an organization development consultant with the Charter Oak Consulting Group, Inc., of Hartford, Connecticut, but she is currently based in Albuquerque, New Mexico. She works with many large corporations by helping them to adjust to the changes they are undergoing as the result of new business strategies and reorganization. She spends a lot of time helping clients find new ways of operating within their newly established parameters. She agreed when I brought up the metaphor of the weaver that she spends a lot of time linking people, ideas, and resources in new ways. "That is what I do a lot of the time when I'm working with clients. It's also what I used to do when I was Assistant Director of Corporate Training for CIGNA. Creating linkages between ideas, between people, and between available resources is often key to my effectiveness with a client."

The more we talked, the more I saw the weaver as Roberta's integrative center of balance in her work. Curious about the extent of the weaver in her life, I asked her what she did while in Bangladesh. "I worked for a women's handicraft training institute where we worked with women in the village in how to make handicrafts more saleable to a Western market, and to charge the right prices. Then those women would go back and take what they had learned and teach other women how to do it. While I was there, I also worked with the World Health Organization on eradicating smallpox and got to see some of the last cases of smallpox in Bangladesh."

The more I listened to Roberta, the clearer it became that the weaver metaphor extended beyond her work into the other aspects of her life as well. "One of the ways I maintain my balance is through keeping connected with the people who are important to me. I call my mother at least once a week, not out of obligation but just to keep in touch. I call my kids, too. I don't just wait for them to call me. Being connected with my husband, Jim, on a daily basis while I'm traveling is essential to me. One friend of mine who was in a consciousness-raising group with me in Bangladesh in 1974 and I have kept up a relationship over the years. Until I moved to New Mexico from Hartford, we'd get together for dinner every six weeks. Those "dinners with Sondra" would get me out of my current focus and help me connect with a part of my life that was very important. Taking care of all sides of myself is important. My work is very demanding but feels very relevant to me, and that for me is critical. I don't think I could do work that I didn't think was meaningful to the people involved.

"Coaching people and helping them grow is really part of my career core. It's certainly part of my role as an external consultant. When I was at CIGNA, I had a staff of six consultants that I coached. Certainly there was a lot of coaching in Bangladesh. I was also a branch director and women's services director at a YWCA. My friends kid me and and say, 'Don't get in a room with Roberta because you'll find yourself connected to someone or something before you leave.' I'm really good at facilitating matches, of networking other people to each other. I guess there's the weaver again.

"On the work scene I spend a tremendous amount of time facilitating the resolution of issues among people. I get a tremendous amount of satisfaction helping people get to solutions that they were unable to come up with on their own. I don't provide the solutions, I just help others find them. I guess there I'm weaving ideas.

"As I think about it, the weaving is a very important part of what I do. It's important for me that when I'm working with a group, whether it's my consulting group, a client group, a political group, or my family, for that matter, that each person in the group leave a situation feeling as if they've gotten what they needed and made a contribution. I like the notion of helping people weave themselves into the fabric of what's going on and finding the strand that works for them."

Tom T.—An Inclination for Innovation

"I don't believe that balanced people get anything done. William Blake said, 'The road of excess leads to the palace of wisdom.' I've always believed in following the road of excess. You can't experience the fullness of life if you're too balanced."

So began my conversation with a man who, I believe, has as the center of his work integration a drive toward innovation. Tom T. is an innovative thinker, businessman, inventor, manager—and entrepreneur. "I was a millionaire, at least on paper, for a short period of time. I lost all that money. That's unfortunate, but I've come to realize that you don't really need money to live. You need creativity, guts, and intuition."

Tom is an entrepreneur in the food industry. "I became interested in nutrition early on in my food career. It's always been important to me that I'm dealing with health food, not junk food. I fancy myself an alchemist. Right now I'm working on creating meat analogs for non–meat-eating Buddhists in Asia, which is an interesting shift for me. In my previous business I took a low-tech product from the Orient, tofu, used American high technology, and then introduced it into a high-tech marketing environment. Now I'm taking a high-tech product—a meat analog—and introducing it in a low-tech arena."

Tom's biggest business innovation to date was the creation and launch of Jofu, a nondairy yogurt substitute made with tofu. The product was eventually sold to a large food manufacturer and is no longer a part of Tom's life. "I was tremendously successful in the short run. The product and its marketing were successful. The problem was that I became too focused on the goal of making money—so much so that I lost sight of my better judgment and trusted the momentum of the business instead of my intuition. I thought I was an independent innovator taking advantage of the financial systems to promote this health food. Instead, the system took advantage of me and left me out of balance.

"Until I was 25, I lived the life of a god. I traveled all over Europe and America and did whatever I wanted on my terms. I did a lot of social kinds of work when I was younger—things that seemed intuitively right. I worked in Harlem and also did some publishing and writing, mostly poetry. I also spent some time at a school for the deaf and blind and worked in a state hospital. I also resisted the draft during the Vietnam War.

"About 15 years ago I started working in the food industry, first with a co-op, then a natural food distributor. In both cases I found that there was a need for the organization to be managed differently or it might fail. Even though I didn't know much about management, I found I had a lot of ideas that worked and could create better conditions for the business to succeed. Eventually I started my first tofu business with a couple of partners, and it was very successful as a cottage industry. From there I started the New England Soy Dairy, where I really became a businessman. We improved technology, wrote business plans, marketing plans, the works. My company eventually became Tomsun Foods International Inc., and attracted a lot of publicity. I made contact with national markets and major food companies. In 1987 the company went public, the national marketing campaign for Jofu began, and we got involved with some financial people whose impatience created problems for us. Eventually I was forced out of the company and found myself looking for some answers, which is when I met you, Neil."

When I met Tom, he was clearly confused about his next steps. He attended my Career Renewal seminar to get a better focus on his skills, talents, and direction. At the end of the series, Tom left with a variety of ideas, each of which sounded creative and innovative. However, I was still not sure which avenue he would pursue. Six months later we met for lunch to touch base. I was curious to see what his innovative mind had come up with. Tom now had nine different ideas, he had developed two partnerships and a consulting business, and he had written half a novel. Yet he still was wondering why he felt fragmented. Amused by his ability to think in boundless terms, I suggested that perhaps what he needed to do was to narrow his focus to one or two of his ideas. I told him that what was throwing him off balance was the scope of his perspective, not the value of his ideas. I left him saying that in six months I would call him again to interview him for my chapter on balance and that I hoped he would be able to offer me a more balanced perspective.

As I sat with Tom during this interview, I found a man who despite his protestations was on the road to balance. "I spend the mornings doing my writing, and I'm having some success getting published. In the afternoon I spend my time developing my new business venture. I have created a vegetarian ham substitute to be widely marketed by partners in Taiwan. We've got a major food company to sponsor us, and in about three weeks we'll be going to Taiwan to do some test marketing. I'm spending time with my kids, beginning to date, and feeling that I'm learning how I want to live."

As I talked with Tom, it seemed to me that for perhaps the first time in his life, at age 45, he is turning his innovative talents toward the management of his own life. When I suggested this to him, he responded strongly. "The turning point for me was when I stopped focusing on my business and started looking at my own life, my values, my personal style, the things that really matter to me. I realized that if I really relied on my creativity, that creativity would support me in every way. That's part of what you would call my career core. Another part of it that I had to accept is that I'm a bit of a gambler. The Hindu religion has a story about the god who created the world that we live in. He is a boy who is a fire god who rolls the dice to make his choices. The metaphor of the youthful fire of creativity and chance is the one that I relate to most."

"Now they say that entrepreneurs are calculated risk takers. I don't believe that. They're possessed people, they're stubborn people, they're passionate, and they love what they're doing. So I think my core is a combination of creativity and passionate risk taking, with an independence hook. Consequently, I'm pretty undaunted by chaos.

"Being open to possibilities is important to me. That's how I got involved in my current business venture. These guys approached me and said, 'Could you develop this product for us in Taiwan?' I said yes before I even knew if I could. Once I got involved with them, I saw that I had the room to create the kind of work day I wanted. So I've been publishing my poetry and am moving forward with product development. I've also found some other people who might be able to use the Taiwan distribution channels we've set up to market other products. A major food company has invested in my new product. I've set up a financial structure so that hopefully my kids will inherit my successes and will be able to build on the business I create. I'm not sure where things are headed, but that's okay. I feel great, I'm bicycling with my kids, I've got some new friends who are really interesting, and I'm taking things as they come. Whatever happens, I'm sure I can handle it and will most likely thrive in it."

BIVOCATIONAL CAREERS

According to a report on the economy of the 1990s by *Fortune* magazine, 80 percent of the new jobs created in the 1990s will be part-time jobs. This may bode well for those who find that in order to achieve the highest level of satisfaction they will have to be bivocational. I use the term "bivocational" to describe those people who find themselves managing two careers at once for the duration of their work lives. These people realize that the nature of their interests, talents, and goals is such that the only way to achieve career satisfaction is to work at two things simultaneously over an extended period. For some people the decision to be bivocational is a reflection of their interests; for others, it's more practical. Some people decide that there are two very different kinds of things that they do well and enjoy doing, while others realize that in order to continue to work in one of their fields they need to do something else to provide them with a base of financial support.

Anne T.—Crunching Numbers and Helping People

When I first met Anne T., she was a highly trained clinical social worker. She had an MSW degree and spent most of her time on the wards of the local psychiatric hospital, helping clinically depressed people struggle through their illness. "Depression is no longer the albatross it once was. People can get help, whether it's through psychological support, through the use of pharmaceuticals that help balance the chemical responses that create the depression or through a variety of other means, and that's exciting." Anne was obviously very skilled and knowledgeable in her field and obviously good at what she did, so I was somewhat puzzled by her expressed discontent about her work. The more we spoke, the more I realized that I was dealing with someone who had to be careful not to "throw the baby out with the bathwater."

When I asked her about her job satisfaction, she said, "I like what I do much of the time. I think I'm a pretty good clinician. The problem is that I also like to see measurable results from my work at least some of the time. When you work with chronically depressed people, most of the time you don't tend to see tangible results. Many people do get better, but it usually takes a while, and you might not even be working with them anymore to see the results. People tend to get moved around the system pretty regularly because of insurance reasons or space availability reasons."

When I asked Anne what other things she might be interested in, she laughed and was hesitant to respond. "I've always been good in math. When I was an undergraduate I would take the most advanced math courses—calculus, trigonometry, advanced statistics—and I would have no trouble getting As. The thing I like about math is its clear-cut nature. You start out with a problem, and you solve it. It's a great feeling, one that I rarely get from the work I do."

In the course of our conversations, I asked Anne if she would be willing to go back to school for the right reasons. She said she would, provided it would help her resolve some of her professional conflicts. As we talked on, I let her know that I thought she might very well be someone who would end up being bivocational. She found the notion interesting once I explained to her what it meant.

Anne did go back to school and got a second bachelor's in accounting. (Her first one had been in psychology.) After extensive planning she decided that her interest in math and her continued interest in clinical psychology did not lend themselves to one career. During her accounting study she met several people who were specializing in tax law. She decided to take some courses to fulfill her nonaccounting requirements and eventually got a job with a tax accounting firm. She is very good at the accounting part and has also developed a specialty, tied to her psychology background, in helping people with math anxiety problems and other related fears do their income taxes. The firm she works with now channels clients to her who feel uneasy divulging to others what many people consider private information. She is very good at making people feel comfortable about the process and will often spend 45 minutes talking with a client about the process before they even open the tax form booklets. She is very busy with her tax work for six months of the year and also sees a few clinical clients when she can. During the off season for taxes, she expands her clinical load and does fill-in work at the psychiatric hospital when they need her. She now describes herself as happily bivocational.

TENSE ANXIETY

"Tense anxiety" refers to problems that emerge from focusing on the past and the future instead of the present. One of the traps many people get into is thinking in the past tense and future tense instead of the present tense. One of the most confusing things about achieving balance is the notion of shifting focus. The passage of time can make it even more difficult. As reflected in many of the stories about balance, it is clear that no one spends his or her life living 20 percent of their time focused on each of the five areas. The reality is that our balance shifts as our lives change. Problems emerge when your focus on any one area is so intense that the other four get neglected for an extended period of time. The 50-year-old career-oriented man who, for the past 20 years, has been neglecting his family in order to further his career is the perfect example of the high cost of a life out of balance. When this man hits, as many men do, a point in his development where relationships become more important than promotions, he may return to his family and say, "I want to get to know you better." The problem is that for the 16-year-old son or daughter whose father has been a stranger for 16 years, the response is often, "Sorry, Dad, it's too late. Where have you been all my life?" The problem here is the man's focus on the future tense. The father, so concerned with career advancement, neglected other important factors and may never be able to regain what he has lost.

Another form of tense anxiety has to do with the person who uses past problems to prevent present and future success. This is the person whose focus on the impact of the past inhibits achievement in the present and future. This problem can take many forms: the person who repeatedly marries the same (wrong) type of person, those who repeatedly take jobs that they don't do well or don't enjoy doing because they believe that's "all they can do," and people who believe they are going to be socially unhappy because "they've always been" all suffer from past tense anxiety.

One of the problems for these people is that they believe they are incapable of change. They believe that they are forever controlled by past decisions and events. Unless you can accept and embrace the notion that balance comes with effectively managing shifting priorities and handling changes as they occur, you are unlikely to achieve the sense of balance everyone needs. Focusing on past failures or future ambitions will heighten your anxiety and prevent you from achieving balance. Focusing on the present will lessen your anxiety, allow you to let go of the past, and help you get what you want in the future. Focusing on the present means more than simply staying in the "here and now." It means paying constant attention to each of the five key elements of balance at all times.

While there may very well be times when some elements

take a back seat to others, keeping each of them in focus will help you prevent losing sight of any of them. Making time to be with your family during particularly hectic work periods, making a quick phone call to work while you're on vacation so you don't spend your free time worrying, and making sure you contribute to causes you care about even when funds are low are all examples of ways you might pay attention to those areas you're not focused on in order to maintain your sense of balance. All the elements of balance need constant attention in order to remain vibrant and not atrophy. This does not mean that you are constantly stretching yourself beyond your limits. On the contrary, it means that you are constantly paying attention to everything that matters so that nothing gets neglected. It is the constant neglect of any element of balance that causes it to decay. Paying careful attention to each area and its needs in the present will ensure that no area suffers from neglect and that you don't get knocked off balance by the absence of balance.

SEVEN

Measuring Your Success

If you are to attain and maintain career wellness, it is critical that you develop ways to monitor your success on an ongoing basis. External changes such as recessions, shifting markets, globalization, and organizational downsizing and restructuring can have an impact on your potential success. Internal changes such as shifts in values, goals, and ambitions can have an impact on your success as well. The person who takes a preventative approach to career wellness anticipates problems and avoids career threats whenever possible. This chapter concerns itself with ways to monitor and measure your success through the use of three devices: the career success time capsule for identifying the parameters for future success, the net satisfaction formula for determining the extent of your current success, and the career success case history for capsulizing the significance of past success. Used carefully, each can provide a barometer for measuring the extent to which you're on the right track and a guide for changing the things that need to be changed.

THE CAREER SUCCESS TIME CAPSULE

As we enter the 1990s, one thing is clear: The notion of career success is becoming increasingly difficult to define. People can no longer measure success the way they used to. Definitions of success are far more personal and far broader than that of the organization man of the 1950s, who measured success by calculating his age times a thousand dollars to see if he was keeping up with his peers. According to David Kirkpatrick, who wrote a cover story for *Fortune* entitled "Is your Career On Track?" "One of the most important changes in the career picture, affecting not just baby boomers but all ages, is occurring not around today's managers but inside them. Personal fulfillment and the flexibility to do more of what one wants are becoming top rank career goals."

Career success is relative. As we've already seen, there used to be distinct ladders to climb and clear-cut ways to measure the extent to which your career was on track. All that has

changed. Large numbers of baby boomers and flattening organizational hierarchies have crowded the rungs of the ladders,
making them obsolete as a measure. The baby bust generation
(those 25 and younger) are challenging the norms and values of
corporate America. Midlife career changers have dispelled the
notion that up is the only way to go. Successful working moth-
ers are proving that there are many ways to maneuver up the
ladder—not just with two hands tightly gripped. Early retirees
are starting new careers and shattering the myth of the serenity
of the golden years. Giving your all is being replaced by balancing your needs.

All this makes the question of your career success a con-
founding one. Since the once all-important dollar (still important) is no longer the standard by which success is measured,
what is a success-oriented professional to do to make sure he or
she is on the road to career wellness?

Here's a simple yet effective way to gauge your career success on an ongoing basis. It is borrowed from the cultural ritual
of the time capsule—a simple metaphoric device used to help a
society convey information about the present to generations of
the future. To use the time capsule to measure your personal
success, you need to be a little creative.

Imagine it's five years in the future (less if your need for
feedback is more pressing). Think about what success at that
future point would look like. Once you have a clear image,
begin gathering artifacts that reflect that image. As you begin
gathering, imagine you are a stranger opening this time capsule. Keep collecting artifacts until you are confident that the
stranger opening your capsule would get a complete idea of
who you are from the contents of the capsule.

Artifacts for your capsule can include written materials, photographs, models, souvenirs, toys, replicas, and the like. For
example, if a new office or new work site is in your plan,
include models. If international experience is part of the plan,
you might throw in a model of the Eiffel Tower, a map of
the Great Wall of China, or a photograph of the Tokyo
Stock Exchange. A nameplate with your new title can invoke
a powerful image, as can a mock-up of your new investment

portfolio. If part of your success is measured by your contribution to others, you may want to create some headlines signaling the eradication of a social ill, for example, "Environment on the Upswing" or "Homelessness Diminishing." While it is unlikely that you would single-handedly be responsible for such a headline, its presence in your capsule will help you measure your contribution.

Once your capsule is complete and you are sure all your measures of success are represented, seal it securely and place it in an inconspicuous place. In a conspicuous place, record the date the capsule is to be opened. When the date arrives, open the capsule. The measure of your career success will be clear.

COWABUNGA DUDE! A NINJA TURTLE TIME CAPSULE

I've used the career success time capsule with many students and clients. The surprising thing to me has been that people didn't have to wait until the opening to get results. The act of filling and sealing the time capsule gave them clarity of vision for their own career management.

Two of my more interesting subjects were Cheryl and Jim Prindle, students in my organizational theory and behavior classes at Cambridge College's Masters in Management program. Cheryl is the executive director of Mirage Studios, birthplace of the Teenage Mutant Ninja Turtles, and Jim is the Turtles' executive director in charge of licensing and merchandising, responsible for marketing the plethora of Ninja Turtle products. When I first met the Prindles, the Ninja Turtle phenomenon was just getting into full swing. The first movie was about to come out, and the studio was growing by leaps and bounds. Kevin Eastman and Peter Laird, creators of the Turtles, were still reeling from the shock of how their black-and-white comic book was blossoming into the hottest thing since Mickey Mouse.

Their assignment was to come into class with the contents of a time capsule ready to be sealed into whatever sort of container they wished. Most people chose a shoebox or something similar, although there were several genie-type bottles, a few L'eggs eggs, and several oversized boxes. The Prindles' container was a medium-sized footlocker with Michaelangelo, Donatello, Raphael, and Leonardo (the Turtles) splashed all over it. When it came to their turn, Cheryl and Jim volunteered (as did five other students) to fill their capsule in front of the entire class. They chose my recommended date of five years and began their presentation. First came memorabilia from the soon-to-be-released *Teenage Mutant Ninja Turtles, The Movie*. Next came a variety of yet-to-be-designed products, including a chain of Turtle Pizza Parlors (the Turtles' favorite food is pizza), cans of Turtle soup, and a variety of other products. Their whole presentation was a model of what an ideal time capsule could be.

When I started writing this section on the career success time capsule, I remembered what an outstanding job the Prindles had done, so I asked them if they would help refresh my memory by opening it prematurely (it had been a year since they had sealed it). We met in the new offices of Mirage Studios on a Saturday morning to review the contents of the capsule and talk about its significance.

"It's very interesting to me that we're doing this today," said Cheryl. "This is my fourth anniversary as executive director of Mirage Studios, and it seems like looking at our progress via the time capsule is an appropriate thing to do."

Jim suggested that we begin by emptying the capsule and putting everything back in with commentary. What follows is a sampling of the items included with accompanying commentary from either Cheryl or Jim:

- A plaque awarded to Cheryl honoring her in *Who's Who of Women Executives*. "I got it this year again and hope to get it for the next five years."

- A Ninja Turtle action figure standing on a globe. "We were hoping for world domination in the toy market. We've been international for a year and a half with products throughout the United States, Canada, Mexico, Australia, Europe, South America, and the Far East."

- A video cassette of a TV ad for a hypothetical Ninja Turtle theme park. "We've just negotiated with Disney to do a Ninja Turtle Pizza Restaurant at both Disneyland and Disney World in 1992."

- A December 13, 1989, issue of *USA Today*, stating that the Turtles had grossed $150 million. "In 1990 that figure jumped to $1.5 billion."

- A bottle of Dom Perignon champagne. "We saw it as a symbol of our need to invest in the future by holding onto valuable items."

- A rubber model of a small, traditional box turtle. "To remind us of our humble beginnings and help us to remember where we came from."

- Behind-the-scenes photos from the first Teenage Mutant Ninja Turtle film, which was about to be released shortly after the closing of the time capsule. "We were hoping this would be the first of many movies. The movie went beyond our expectations and turned out to be the fourth-largest box office hit of 1990."

- A December 12, 1989, issue of the *Wall Street Journal* with a picture of a Teenage Mutant Ninja Turtle action figure on the front page, predicting the Turtles would be the biggest-selling Christmas toy of the 1989 season. "It was a nice Christmas present for us and a sign that we were here to stay. A recent toy fair predicted we would also be the biggest selling toy in 1991."

- A picture of an overseas foster child, one of two Cheryl has currently. "I hope to adopt a child some day, but for now these are my children."

- A picture of their recently purchased condominium. "We live a low-key life-style, and that's important to us. We've stopped telling people what we do for a living because the reactions are hard to handle and it can get uncomfortable."

While many other artifacts were included, the list represents the range of items the Prindles chose. With more than 1,500 licensees to manage, the Prindles are clearly running a company with a bright future. Every indication is that their products will continue to thrive in the marketplace. I asked them if they found any particular value in doing the time capsule activity. "I wish I had thought to do this in the early days," said Cheryl. "I was here when it was just comic books. It would have been nice to see what I envisioned back then when we were in our 900-square-foot office trying to make ends meet, as opposed to the 10,000 square feet we're in now with all our success."

"It's good to be able to pull the time capsule out," said Jim, "and say, 'what were we thinking, why did we put these things in there.' It gives you a nice perspective on where you were and what you'd done to get there. It's also good for memories. While not everyone would have the kinds of things we had to put in, I think it's a way for people to preserve things that are important to them. What you put in is very significant and says a lot about what's important to you."

"The capsule helps us focus on our personal goals in relationship to the business." said Cheryl. "We have things like marketing plans, but we're very busy and it's easy to get off track. The capsule helps focus you because it asks the question very vividly, 'Where do you want to be in five years?' Your answers help keep you on track."

"You have to be sincere and honest with yourself when doing it," Jim said. "You have to think about it carefully and put things in that have meaning to you and will have meaning in the future when you open it up."

"We took a lot of time doing it," Cheryl said. "We looked around the house for significant items, then we looked around the office and the stock room. Then we sat down and thought very philosophically about things. I would like to think that in five years Ninja Turtles will be on people's minds as much as they are now because then I'll know that we've become a classic like Mickey Mouse and Bugs Bunny—and there's nothing more flattering or more gratifying to us than knowing you've created characters that kids identify with and have so much fun with."

"We've decided to open the capsule once a year and keep adding to it until the five years are up and then start another one," said Jim. "I'm planning to go to law school," said Cheryl. "I think I'll put a mock-up of my law degree in there."

"My hometown just did a 100-year time capsule and put my high school picture, a Ninja Turtle figure, and some articles about me in it," Jim said. "I think I'm going to take the clipping about their time capsule and put that in our time capsule."

"We value the capsule very much now," said Cheryl. "We've moved twice since we did it, and we've taken great care to see that it didn't get damaged. I think everyone who wants to monitor their progress should do one."

Since initially developing the idea of the time capsule, I've expanded it to include not just work-related artifacts but also items that reflect the importance of balance (as discussed in Chapter 6) by including artifacts from the other four elements as well. Many people, like Cheryl and Jim, included them already. Following are some ideas to help you think about the types of items you might include in your capsule (should you decide to do it) that reflect each of the five key elements of a balanced life.

Work Artifacts   These items should reflect the nature of your work, your level of responsibility, and the setting in which you work and should include any items that help to identify the work you do in terms of work processes, tasks, and outcomes. Items might include such things as nameplates, equipment, reports, wardrobe items, products, and models of buildings or offices.

Family and Friends Artifacts   When thinking about artifacts that reflect this area, think about your immediate family and your close circle of friends. What's important here is to focus on those people you see as contributing to your having a successful family and social life. If you have children, you may want to think about the role you are going to play in their lives over the next few years and symbols that reflect your roles. If you're single and unattached, you may want to think about the extent to which you want to be involved with other people and the nature of those relationships. If you're in a family situation, dolls representing new family members, trip tickets, a model of a new home, and symbols of family member accomplishments (such as degrees and awards) may be included in your capsule. If you're single and unattached, items symbolizing social clubs, prospective partners, or your personal support network might be appropriate.

Play and Recreation Artifacts Here you should focus on the kinds of things you are going to do for pleasure. To get a complete view of this area, think about those things you do now that bring you pleasure, as well as those you would like to do that you haven't been doing. You could, at this point, commit yourself to doing more of the things you enjoy but have been neglecting. For example, you may decide to set a "playtime goal" to attend a concert, movie, or sports event at least once a month. You might include sports trophies, exercise equipment, club memberships, and hobby items as well.

Learning Artifacts When thinking about time capsule contents for learning, you may decide to include items that reflect formal learning situations such as degrees, certificates, diplomas, or courses taken. If your learning goals do not lend themselves to such a structured approach in that you don't plan on going to school or taking courses, you might want to think about ways in which you hope to grow and develop and include items that reflect new skills learned, experiences gained, or challenges met. For these types of learning situations, you might include objects that reflect the learning, such as computer disks, books, and models of tools or equipment.

Social Responsibility Artifacts Here you want to focus on what you plan to do to respond to social needs. If you plan to commit time to working for a particular cause, you may want to set a target that reflects improvement in that area. If you plan to contribute primarily through financial support, you may want to indicate the extent of your commitment. For example, some people commit a certain percentage of their income to social contribution. If you have a goal in this area, you may want to include it. This is also the place you may want to identify your involvement in eradicating social problems through organized activities, including church groups or social action committees. Your artifacts in this area might include civic awards, headlines reflecting volunteer experience, petitions, letters of commendation, or objects reflecting progress in the areas you intend to work on. Some people, not prone to thinking in terms of social responsibility, have trouble identifying a cause that would inspire them to action. The following scenario sometimes helps. Imagine you were to win the lottery. Your attorney tells you that in order to make the most of your winnings you need to contribute $1 million to a worthy cause. Which cause would you choose to help with your contribution? Your response to this will likely help you identify which causes you may want to help and include in your time capsule.

Complete the success time capsule seriously and thoroughly, and chances are good you'll gain a clearer sense of your goals and how to meet them. Pay attention to what you're doing, and you'll also gain a more focused view of those aspects of your life that are currently working to your satisfaction and those that need further attention in order to make you feel more successful and more satisfied in both the near and distant future.

DETERMINING YOUR NET SATISFACTION

While the career success time capsule can help you determine steps toward future satisfaction, it's also important to consider your present satisfaction. The net satisfaction formula can help you assess your current level of satisfaction. It is based on the extent to which your current work matches your values, is moving you toward your goals, and is utilizing your strongest abilities. Like "net worth," which gives you the bottom line after all the pluses and minuses have been factored in, net satisfaction gives you a gauge of how satisfied you are with your current work.

To determine your net satisfaction, you need to sort out the three key variables: values, goals, and abilities. The first thing to consider is values: Take a moment and think about the five things that are most satisfying about your work (such as the money, sense of accomplishment, security, or ability to learn new things). Next, think about the five things that you want that you don't have and that contribute to your dissatisfaction (for example, the money, lack of opportunity, or work environment). List these items on a piece of paper in any order. Assign them a weight of importance by rating each value you are satisfied with on a scale of +1 to +10 (for instance, if you make a lot of money and are satisfied with the amount, give that item a value of +10). Next rate each value you are dissatisfied with on a scale of −1 to −10 (if you hate your work environment and feel strongly about it, give it a rating of −10). When you've finished rating each of the ten items, calculate your score for the values variable. Be sure you include your minus signs in your calculations. When you're done you should have a score ranging from +45 to −45.

Next, focus on goals. For this you need to think about where you're headed and where you want to be in the future. Choose a period for which you want to measure your current satisfaction, anywhere from one year to five years in the future. Once you've picked a point in time, think about where you want to be by then, and write down three goals that reflect that target (such as, "I want to be making $75,000 a year within two years," or "I want to be head of my department within three years"). Next, consider each of the three goals, and rate your chances of reaching them. Give each goal a rating of 1, 5, or 10. If you believe your current work is unlikely to help you to meet the goal, give it a 1. If you think it is somewhat likely to help you, give it a 5. If you believe your current work is highly likely to help you reach your goal, give it a 10. When you're done adding, you should have a "goals" score between 3 and 30.

Next you need to consider abilities. Take a moment and write down your five strongest skills. Then consider the extent to which your current work requires you to use each of these skills in what you do. For each skill, assign a number from 1 to 5. If you use that skill a little or not at all, give it a 1. If you use that skill a fair amount, give it a 3. If you use that skill a lot, give it a 5. When you're done, add up your "skills" score. You should have a total of between 5 and 25.

Next, you need to add up your scores from the three sections: Your values score (between +45 and −45), your goals score (between 3 and 30), and your abilities score (between 5 and 25).

When you are done you should have a total score between −37 and +100. The following interpretation of your scores will determine your net satisfaction and your urgency in making a career or job change:

A score of 75 to 100 suggests that your net satisfaction is high. There may be some things about your work that you don't like, but the indicators suggest that you are in a situation that is providing you with what you want, moving you toward your goals, and utilizing your greatest strengths.

A score of 50 to 74 suggests that while some of your needs are being met, there's a lot missing as well. Important here is that you not "throw the baby out with the bathwater" and give up important things in the process. If you decide to make a move, make sure you're not going to be giving up more than you're gaining.

A score of 0 to 49 is dangerously low in that you're probably not getting what you need and want, are not moving in your desired direction, and are most likely not using your greatest strengths. You should strongly consider a change in jobs or a change in career.

A score below zero is a real warning signal. Chances are if you scored this low, your work is creating tremendous amounts of stress and dissatisfaction. You should be considering strategies for making a change and doing all you can to get into a more satisfying position.

The basic assumption of the net satisfaction formula is that in order for your career to thrive, you need to be experiencing a certain level of satisfaction that comes from getting what you want, moving toward your goals, and utilizing your talents. The absence of a reasonably good net satisfaction score suggests it's time for you to make a change. The kind of change you make should be determined by the nature and source of the dissatisfaction. If important values are not being satisfied, this may mean renegotiating responsibilities or it may mean changing the nature of what you do entirely. If the likelihood of goals being met is small, it may mean a reassessment of your potential or a shift in your strategy. If your talents are not being utilized, it may mean you need to inform and persuade others to use you more effectively, or it may mean that your job and you are mismatched.

Use your net satisfaction score and analysis of your scoring to determine your career strategy and you'll be less likely to feel bankrupted by your low value in what is an invaluable commodity in your career—your satisfaction.

CAREER SUCCESS CASE HISTORY

Focusing on the future and the present are far more important than dwelling on the past. That's why I urge you to use the career success time capsule and the net satisfaction formula. The first will help you set targets for future success; the second will help you gauge your current success. There are times, however, when focusing on past successes can give you insight into your current endeavors and serve as a motivator for future ambitions. If you feel that you could use either of these things, complete a career success case history. It's very simple to do. Begin by listing each of the positions you've held throughout your career. Once you have your list, think about the one thing you did while you held each position that you feel most proud of, the thing that you believe best highlights your competence. Write it down on a piece of paper and describe what it was that you contributed that made the endeavor successful. Do this with each of the positions you've held, going as far back as you wish, and you'll find yourself with a case history rich with data, one that reminds you of your strengths and boosts your confidence. Incidentally, these descriptions of successes can be a substantive addition to your resume, should you decide to include them under your description of each position you've held. Remember, focusing on the past here is fruitful only if it adds to your sense of success in the present or motivates you toward reaching success in the future.

Most important in all of this is to recognize that your career—and your career wellness—exists on a continuum. While you don't want to feel locked in and limited by your past career experience, you do want to tap the successes of your past to fuel the present and propel you into your desired future. Your skills and talents don't exist in a vacuum; they are the accumulation of all you've done in your working life. Consider your past successes and your current efforts as investments in your targeted future, and you're more likely to make the most of your career.

Epilogue

Career management is such a complex and personal thing that I undoubtedly have overlooked some questions that you might have. I hope I have covered enough issues that are important to you so that you feel more capable of anticipating, preventing, and overcoming the problems that come your way. I hope as well that you have further developed your own abilities to think like a career doctor, which is ultimately the best way to maintain a healthy career. Remember that diagnosis is the key to solving the kinds of problems that can plague your career and that accurate diagnosis and early treatment can prevent unnecessary complications. Remember also that prevention can make all the difference in the life of your career. Find ways to balance career and other areas of your life and find ways to balance all the key variables within your work. Be sure to keep an eye on your progress by periodically measuring your success, and be sure to choose new paths when the old ones grow too wearying. Most important, be sure to enjoy your career, for that is surely the key to your success. I wish you good luck and career wellness.

~ ~ ~

Dr. Neil Yeager presents lectures and seminars and consults in a variety of areas, including career management, organization development, risk taking, managing change, mentoring, and leadership. For more information, call or write:

Neil Yeager
P.O. Box 592
N. Amherst, MA 01059
(413) 545-1957

INDEX